HOW THE COMMUNIST MANIFESTO OF 1848 BLUEPRINTS THE ACTIONS OF THE DEMOCRATIC PARTY AND PRESIDENT OBAMA TODAY

UNDERMINING THE U.S. CONSTITUTION

Diane S. Vann

authorHOUSE®

AuthorHouse™
1663 Liberty Drive
Bloomington, IN 47403
www.authorhouse.com
Phone: 1-800-839-8640

Published by AuthorHouse 12/11/2012

ISBN: 978-1-4678-7143-3 (sc)
ISBN: 978-1-4678-7144-0 (e)
ISBN: 978-1-4772-6397-6 (audio)

Library of Congress Control Number: 2011961028

Contents

Communist Manifesto Opposes Constitution

The Constitution was the result of the maturing of the thoughts and ideas put forward by many different outstanding people. They were people with varying levels of education, who knew from experience what they did not want in government. They knew what it was like to have their hopes and dreams limited by the social status of their birth and by the intrusion of government.

After rejecting England's monarch, our founding fathers "brain stormed" together on what government would work best for all people. Their ideas centered on their shared belief in the existence of a power greater than them. In the Declaration of Independence they asserted that all men are created equal and endowed by their Creator with unalienable rights neither transferable to nor deniable by man. After weighing pros and cons for a democracy or a republic, they chose the republic. A pure democracy is government by the majority (or mob rule) while a republic is government that protects the minority from the majority.

Practical experience came from the implementation in 1781 of the first Constitution, the Articles of Confederation. The second and final Constitution, signed by 39 delegates on September 17, 1787, delineated a representative republic with three branches of government (legislative, executive, and judicial) and an amendment process. The amendment process, the "living part" of the Constitution, alters the Constitution when needed but never erases it.

The Constitution places ultimate power in the hands of the voters rather than the elected. It protects our individual rights. Following the Constitution made the United States of America the primary leader of the free world. Our nation has prospered and been blessed by God. When called upon by other nations in wars or famines, we helped them.

The United States of America (USA), because of the Constitution, nurtures what Karl Marx called "capitalism," where private individuals and corporations invest in and own the means of production and distribution rather than government. Capitalism produces competition that breeds the incentive to be creative and improve things. Individuals in the USA have the freedom to choose what they will do; for example, one can choose to spend one's life working to accumulate money or working as a nurse.

The Communist Manifesto was written by Karl Marx and Frederick or Friedrich Engels in 1847-8 for people who were knowledgeable about and directly opposed to America's founding fathers' beliefs and the Constitution. (Within the manifesto America is referred to five times and the word constitution is mentioned three). The manifesto is a detailed prescription for bringing down advanced countries like the USA. In brief, the prescription is for Communists of the working class to first take over a political party, gain control of the government, and then bring the ruling middle class and government down with the help of trade unions and socialists. The desired outcome of the prescription is that no class will oppress another and everyone's status will be equal, even though only the Communists will know the ultimate plan for the worldwide government. There is no further description of the future, which is left as a utopian void to be filled in by the Communists. (W. Cleon Skousen described in 1958 in his book The Naked Communist the atheistic "Communist dictatorship" that resulted in nations that followed Marx's prescription).

Andrew Jackson (1767-1845), the 7th president of the United States from 1829-37, signed into law the Indian Removal Act on May 28, 1830. The Democratic Party of the USA, the oldest existing Democratic Party in the world, was started in 1828-32 to aid in Jackson's reelection. Following his landslide reelection, Native American Indians without hope left their lands and possessions in the states of Georgia, Alabama, North Carolina, Tennessee and Texas. They were relocated to the Indian Territory (now Oklahoma). More than 4,000 lost their lives on the "Trail of Tears." Proceeds from the sale of the Indian lands went to the federal treasury to settle the government's debt.

According to Marx and Engels in 1848, "the theory of the Communists may be summed up in the single sentence: Abolition of private property." President Jackson personified that theory when he enforced the Indian Removal Act. Their approval of Jackson's actions may be at least in part, if not all, of the reason why they wrote near the end of the Communist Manifesto that "In short, the Communists. . . . labor everywhere for the union and agreement of the democratic parties of all countries." (The term democrat was used a total of three times in the Communist Manifesto: one time in "Social-Democrat;" one time in "Democratic Socialists;" and one time in "the democratic parties." All three were in the last section, Section 4).

Norman Mattoon Thomas (1884-1968), six time candidate for president of the United States, reportedly said in a speech in 1944 that "The American people will never knowingly adopt socialism. But, under the name of 'liberalism,' they will adopt every fragment of the socialist program, until one day America will be a socialist nation, without knowing how it happened." Then later he said "I no longer need to run as a Presidential Candidate for the Socialist Party. The Democrat Party has adopted our platform."

The Democratic Socialists of America (DSA) is the United States (U.S.) democratic socialist organization affiliated with the Socialist International. The Socialist International is a federation of democratic socialist, social democratic, social progressive, labor parties and organizations. In October 2009, the DSA released a newsletter listing 70 members of the 111th U.S. Congress as DSA members. All but Senator Bernie Sanders, an Independent from Vermont, were members of the Democratic Party. All but 7 were reelected in 2010 to the 112th Congress.

The Communist Party USA officially endorsed President Barack Obama for the 2012 election on August 4, 2011.

In contrast, the Republican Party was organized in 1854-56 for opposing the extension of slavery. Abraham Lincoln (1809-1865), President of the United States (1861-65) during the Civil War, being advised by fellow Republican and former slave Frederick Douglass, issued the Emancipation Proclamation (Jan. 1, 1863) freeing all slaves in those states fighting the union. Lincoln also pressed for the 13th Amendment barring slavery forever. It was ratified and added to the Constitution on December 6, 1865 following Lincoln's April 15th assassination.

Today the Democratic Party is expert in distracting Americans from its historical and current actions by projecting them onto the Republican Party. Their "devious manipulation" of history and language in regard to black Americans is well documented in the 2011 book Frederick Douglass Republicans: The Movement to Re-Ignite America's Passion for Liberty by K. Carl Smith with his brother Dr. Karnie C. Smith, Sr.

The Real Communist Threat Witnessed

MY EXPERIENCE IN COMMUNIST EAST BERLIN & FREE WEST BERLIN IN 1977

I am a Vietnam era veteran, and I was last posted as a registered nurse on active duty in the United States Army Reserve Nurse Corps to 2nd General Hospital, Landstuhl, Germany in 1975. During our orientation we were asked to visit East Germany (the German Democratic Republic or GDR) because Communists were telling East Germans that the American military were leaving West Germany (the Federal Republic of Germany or FRG). We were told to "wear your uniform so you will not be shot as a spy."

When World War II ended in Europe in 1945, Germany was split from north to south. The capital Berlin fell to the east of the new boundary also known as (AKA) the "Iron Curtain." Too important to cede to one side, Berlin was split into four occupied sectors. The American, British, and French sectors (AKA West Berlin) were administered by the Allies on a rotating basis. The Soviet sector (AKA East Berlin) was administered by the Soviet Union.

So in July of 1977, shortly before I was due to come home, I flew 100 miles behind the Iron Curtain to West Berlin. After finding a place to stay and touring West Berlin, I toured East Berlin by bus and then by foot via Checkpoint Charlie. After a few days I departed West Berlin on the "troop train," an overnight trip that took 9 hours because every 20 miles the train was stopped for the East German engineers to be exchanged, so they could not collude and escape with the train again. So why would anyone try to escape the utopia foretold in the Communist Manifesto or Manifesto of the Communist Party?

I found West Berlin to be very upbeat with lots of people, vehicles, stores, and colorful signs in evidence. Only one building, a church, was left with its bullet ridden walls unchanged as a memorial to World War II (the Kaiser Wilhelm Memorial). I rode public transportation and was handed a leaflet advertising a Communist demonstration which I saw and photographed later.

East Berlin was a very different story. It was depressingly quiet with very few vehicles and without colorful signs. People I walked by on my solo walking tour stared without returning my smile. A memorable statue downtown was a roughly three story high, stooped over workman wearing a huge frown with a sickle on his back.

President Barack Obama's speeches as a presidential candidate reminded me of the prepared speech of the middle aged, East Berlin guide who got on my tour bus at the Communist end of Checkpoint Charlie. Obama's communist agenda matches what I heard and witnessed that day and has inspired me to write this book for my fellow noncommunist Americans.

As we drove through East Berlin's streets, still bombed out and shot up 32 years post World War II, our guide listed problems like the need for more housing that the government was going to solve. Problems that I knew were well in hand on the free West Berlin side. Her rehearsed delivery of the utopian changes to come because of government made me think that she was brain washed.

Then we stopped for a bite to eat at a small cafeteria. I, an almost 25 year old uniformed United States Army officer, was sitting at a table with a middle aged stranger. Our tour guide confidently sat down with us and began to share how much she and her family hated living in East Germany, how her children were in trouble at school because they preferred learning English to Russian as their second language, and how her husband could leave the country to attend medical conferences but they could not accompany him.

Afterwards I was thinking that she was definitely not brain washed, and I was surprised when the stranger at the table said "That is the stupidest woman you will ever meet in your life." When I asked why, he stated "Either one of us could have been a plant." He explained that in World War II he was a spy in Berlin for the Allies, and now he was on his first visit "to see the changes."

West Berlin's Overlook of the Berlin Wall

The Berlin Wall was built in 1961 in the former Potsdamer Platz (pictured above on the side of West Berlin's overlook of the Berlin Wall) by East Germany to stop people from leaving the Communist controlled east side for the Western controlled west side. Following this paragraph are copies of my travel orders and the pictures taken with my small Kodak 110 camera on July 31-Aug 2, 1977. Their captions are the brief descriptions I wrote on their backs (Brandenburger Tor is the German name for the Brandenburg Gate).

UNITED STATES OF AMERICA
ÉTATS-UNIS D'AMERIQUE
СОЕДИНЕННЫЕ ШТАТЫ АМЕРИКИ

MOVEMENT ORDERS
LAISSEZ-PASSER
ПУТЕВКА

Name Nom, Prénom Фамилия, Имя	Rank Qualité Чин	Nationality Nationalité Гражданство	Identity Document No. Pièce d'identité No. № удостоверения личности
SWANSON DIANE E	1LT USAR	American	

is / are authorized to travel from
est / sont autorisé(s) à se rendre de
уполномочен/уполномочены
следовать из
to Helmstedt à and return
et retour
в Berlin и обратно

by train or by vehicle No.
par le train ou par voiture No.
поездом или на автомашине №

from (date)   16 Jul 77   to (date)   14 Aug 77   inclusive
du (date)   au (date)   inclus
от (число)   по (число)   включительно

by
par

The Commander-in-Chief of the United States Army, Europe
Le Commandant-en-Chef de l'Armée Americaine en Europe
Главнокомандующим Американской Армии в Европе.

Signature   *Guy F. Cardinalli*
Подпись

Title   GUY F. CARDINALLI
Qualité   COL, AGC
Звание   Asst Adjutant General

Date   1 6 JUL 1977
Число

Front of Military Orders

TRAVEL INSTRUCTIONS   ORDRE DE ROUTE   КОМАНДИРОВКА

SWANSON DIANE E   1LT USAR

will proceed without restriction to and from Berlin in
connection with the occupation of Berlin.

se rendra/rendront à Berlin et en reviendra/reviendront, sans
aucune limitation, pour des motifs afférents à l'occupation de
la ville.

проследует беспрепятственно в Берлин и обратно в связи
с оккупацией Берлина.

Valid for one round trip

Valable pour un voyage aller et retour

Действительна на одну поездку туда и обратно

from   to   inclusive.
du   16 Jul 77   au   14 Aug 77   inclus.
от_____ по_____ включительно.
            (date)
            (число)

Issued on   1 6 JUL 1977
Délivré le
Выдано (число)

Signature
Подпись

Title   GUY F. CARDINALLI
Qualité   COL, AGC
Звание   Asst Adjutant General

Back of Military Orders

East Berlin July '77 me Graveyard Memorial to Soviet soldiers killed in World
War II. Twin Stone Monuments to represent Soviet Red Flags

The Wall -- Barbed Wire and Mine Fields -- Looking Out at Berlin's Former
Potsdamer Platz from West Berlin

The Wall from West Berlin--In distance--east side--green roof of bunker where
Hitler committed suicide

The Wall West Berlin July '77

"Warning: You're Now Leaving West Berlin." Brandenburger Tor from West July '77

West Berlin July '77 River Spree separating East & West Berlin--graves of East Germans who tried to escape across water

West Berlin Looking from Wittenburg Platz to the Kaiser Wilhelm Memorial

Brandenburger Tor built late 18th century on model of Propylaea in Athens as seen from East Berlin 2 Aug 77

East Berlin 31 July '77

INTRODUCTION TO THE
COMMUNIST MANIFESTO

*C*ontrary to what some people believe, Communism's threat to the United States (US) did not vanish with the disintegration of the Union of Soviet Socialist Republics (USSR). There is no excuse for willful ignorance of this fact. A quote attributed to Nikita Khrushchev, a leader of the USSR in the mid 20th century, is: "We can't expect the American People to jump from Capitalism to Communism, but we can assist their elected leaders in giving them small doses of Socialism, until they awaken one day to find that they have Communism."

I believe that every American should read and understand the Communist Manifesto, because that knowledge is the key to our nation's long term defense. Due to its public domain status, the Communist Manifesto is not protected by copyright laws. The text of the entire pamphlet (without any prefaces and footnotes by Karl Marx and Frederick Engels) follows next in this book. To make it easier to get through, I ***underline and italicize*** the points I feel are most critical and add explanatory remarks in **bold Andy font.**

German members of the Communist League in England contracted in 1847 with Karl Marx to write the Communist Manifesto for them. He wrote it in the German language with input from his friend Frederick Engels. It was first published in German in England in February 1848.

Karl Marx reportedly grew up in an upper class family and was college educated in his homeland Germany (then Prussia). Forgoing a working class job, he lived off the proceeds of his incendiary Socialist writings and was driven out of Germany as well as other countries. Settling finally in England, there were times he could not leave his home because he had pawned his clothes. Three of his children died because he did not pay for their medicine.

Reading Marx's prescription for bringing down an advanced capitalist country is not easy. I was tempted to rip it up the first 6 times I read it. Also, *it is not well written and for that I blame Marx and not the translators. Marx wrote under the pressure of time and probably with limited paper and ink, so most of his critical points are written in throwaway lines. Subsequent Communist writers continue to embellish on his points.*

In his first section, Marx reduces all history to class warfare and details the two main classes of his (and our) day. The oppressor "ruling" class is the capitalist class which he calls the "bourgeois." The oppressed class is the working class which he calls the "proletarian." To be fair, his 1st section makes some valid observations about living conditions at his time, which was nearer the onset of the industrial age. In his 2nd section Marx describes the relationship of Communists to Proletarians. Communists, as a working-class party, are proletarians who "clearly understand the . . . ultimate general results of the proletarian movement . . . . summed up in the single sentence: Abolition of private property." The end of section 2 is the easiest part of the manifesto to read. There Marx numbered 1—10 ten interventions for bringing about the downfall of advanced capitalist countries. In his 3rd section, Marx does a review of the Socialist and Communist literature. He details the different Socialist parties of the day and their usefulness to Communists. In his short 4th section, Marx emphasizes that Communists should use various existing opposition parties for Communist purposes, and he calls on the democratic parties and working men of all countries to unite.

It is remarkable that Marx excluded mention of the slavery of his day, referring to it only as if it was in the distant past(i.e., in the "history of all hitherto existing societies" and "in ancient Rome"). Instead he equated the oppression of the working class by the middle class to the oppression of the slave by the slave owner. He took the real life experiences of Africans sold into slavery in America and substituted the word proletarian for African and bourgeoisie for slave owner (e.g., "all family ties among the proletarians are torn asunder" and "bourgeois society ought long ago to have gone to the dogs through sheer idleness").

It is also notable that Marx, after assessing all of the parties of the day in 1848, selected the democratic party to advance the Communist agenda. The Democratic Party of the USA, the oldest existing in the world, was started in 1828-32 to aid in the reelection of our 7th president, Andrew Jackson. President Andrew Jackson is infamous for enforcing the Indian Removal Act which he signed into law May 28, 1830.

Within the text of the Communist Manifesto, Marx takes positions in direct opposition to those taken by the authors of the Constitution of the United States. He is dismissive of political constitutions (e.g., "Into their place stepped free competition, accompanied by a social and political constitution adapted to it, and by the economical and political sway of the bourgeois class") and he is dismissive of family, country, law, morality and religion (e.g., "Law, morality, religion, are to him so many bourgeois prejudices"). Marx's Communist Manifesto is, essentially, the antithesis of the Constitution of the United States.

Diane Vann

From "Introduction" by Francis B. Randall, Sarah Lawrence College, page 25 of <u>The Communist Manifesto, Karl Marx and Friedrich Engels; the Revolutionary Economic, Political, and Social Treatise That Has Transfigured the World</u>:

At a time when most European countries were still ruled, or at least co-ruled, by kings and nobles, Marx had the vision to see that the bourgeoisie was taking over. "Bourgeoisie" had originally meant the inhabitants of cities, but by the Romantic age the term had come to mean the middle classes, whether they lived in cities or not. Businessmen from the greatest textile magnates to the smallest hole-in-the-wall shopkeepers, doctors, lawyers, teachers and other educated and professional people, all the groups that we now call "white collar workers" were part of the bourgeoisie. Marx often felt compelled to give a narrow economic definition of the ***bourgeoisie***--"the owners of the means of capitalist production"--but he used the term to indicate the ***middle classes as a whole.***

Preceding quote from: <u>**The Communist Manifesto, Karl Marx and Friedrich Engels; the Revolutionary Economic, Political, and Social Treatise That Has Transfigured the World,**</u> translation by Samuel Moore, edited by Joseph Katz, copyrighted 1964.

For background material read **Marx for Beginners,** by Rius.

THE COMMUNIST MANIFESTO

ALSO KNOWN AS (AKA) "TRASHING OF THE AMERICAN DREAM" & "KILLING THE GOOSE THAT LAID THE GOLDEN EGG"*

By Karl Marx and Frederick Engels

*<u>Underlining</u> and **Notes in Andy font** added by Diane Vann

Introduction

Aspectre is haunting Europe -- the specter of Communism. All the Powers of old Europe have entered into a holy alliance to exorcise this specter: Pope and Czar, Metternich and Guizot, French Radicals and German police-spies.

Where is the party in opposition that has not been decried as Communistic by its opponents in power? Where is the Opposition that has not hurled back the branding reproach of Communism, against the more advanced opposition parties, as well as against its reactionary adversaries?

Two things result from this fact.

I. Communism is already acknowledged by all European Powers to be itself a Power.

II. It is high time that Communists should openly, in the face of the whole world, publish their views, their aims, their tendencies, and meet this nursery tale of the Specter of Communism with a Manifesto of the party itself.

To this end, Communists of various nationalities have assembled in London, and sketched the following Manifesto, to be published in the English, French, German, Italian, Flemish and Danish languages.

Section I. Bourgeois and Proletarians

The *history of all hitherto existing societies is the history of class struggles.*

Freeman and slave, patrician and plebeian, lord and serf, guild-master and journeyman, in a word, *oppressor and oppressed*, stood in constant opposition to one another, carried on an uninterrupted, now hidden, now open fight, a fight that each time ended, either in a revolutionary reconstitution of society at large, or in the common ruin of the contending classes.

In the earlier epochs of history, we find almost everywhere a complicated arrangement of society into various orders, a manifold gradation of social rank. In ancient Rome we have patricians, knights, plebeians, slaves; in the Middle Ages, feudal lords, vassals, guild-masters, journeymen, apprentices, serfs; in almost all of these classes, again, subordinate gradations.

The modern bourgeois society that has sprouted from the ruins of feudal society has not done away with class antagonisms. It has but established new classes, new conditions of oppression, new forms of struggle in place of the old ones. ***Our epoch***, the epoch of the bourgeoisie, possesses, however, this distinctive feature: it has simplified the class antagonisms: Society as a whole is more and more splitting up into two great hostile camps, into ***two great classes***, directly facing each other: ***Bourgeoisie and Proletariat***.

From the serfs of the Middle Ages sprang the chartered burghers of the earliest towns. From these burgesses the first elements of the bourgeoisie were developed.

The discovery of America, the rounding of the Cape, opened up fresh ground for the rising bourgeoisie. The East-Indian and Chinese markets, the colonization of America, trade with the colonies, the increase in the means of exchange and in commodities generally, gave to commerce, to navigation, to industry, an impulse never before known, and thereby, to the revolutionary element in the tottering feudal society, a rapid development.

The feudal system of industry, under which industrial production was monopolized by closed guilds, now no longer sufficed for the growing wants of the new markets. The manufacturing system took its place. The guild-masters were pushed on one side by the manufacturing middle class; division of labor between the different corporate guilds vanished in the face of division of labor in each single workshop.

Meantime the markets kept ever growing, the demand ever rising. Even manufacture no longer sufficed. Thereupon, steam and machinery revolutionized industrial production. The place of manufacture was taken by the giant, Modern Industry, the place of the industrial middle class, by industrial millionaires, the leaders of whole industrial armies, the modern bourgeois.

Modern industry has established the world-market, for which the discovery of America paved the way. This market has given an immense development to commerce, to navigation, to communication by land. This development has, in its time, reacted on the extension of industry; and in proportion as industry, commerce, navigation, railways extended, in the same proportion the bourgeoisie developed, increased its capital, and pushed into the background every class handed down from the Middle Ages.

We see, therefore, how the modern bourgeoisie is itself the product of a long course of development, of a series of revolutions in the modes of production and of exchange.

Each step in the development of the bourgeoisie was accompanied by a corresponding political advance of that class. An oppressed class under the sway of the feudal nobility, an armed and self-governing association in the mediaeval commune; here independent urban republic (as in Italy and Germany), there taxable "third estate" of the monarchy (as in France), afterwards, in the period of manufacture proper, serving either the semi-feudal or the absolute monarchy as a counterpoise against the nobility, and, in fact, corner-stone of the great monarchies in general, the bourgeoisie has at last, since the establishment of Modern Industry and of the world-market, conquered for itself, in the modern representative State, exclusive political sway. The executive of the modern State is but a committee for managing the common affairs of the whole bourgeoisie.

The bourgeoisie, historically, has played a most revolutionary part.

The bourgeoisie, wherever it has got the upper hand, has put an end to all feudal, patriarchal, idyllic relations. It has pitilessly torn asunder the motley feudal ties that bound man to his "natural superiors," and has left remaining no other nexus between man and man than naked self-interest, than callous "cash payment." It has drowned the most heavenly ecstasies of religious fervor, of chivalrous enthusiasm, of philistine sentimentalism, in the icy water of egotistical calculation. It has resolved personal worth into exchange value, and in place of the numberless and feasible chartered freedoms, has set up that single, unconscionable freedom -- ***Free Trade***. In one word, for exploitation, veiled by religious and political illusions, naked, shameless, direct, brutal ***exploitation***.

The bourgeoisie has stripped of its halo every occupation hitherto honored and looked up to with reverent awe. It has converted the physician, the lawyer, the priest, the poet, the man of science, into its paid wage laborers.

The bourgeoisie has torn away from the family its sentimental veil, and has reduced the family relation to a mere money relation.

The bourgeoisie has disclosed how it came to pass that the brutal

21

display of vigor in the Middle Ages, which Reactionists so much admire, found its fitting complement in the most slothful indolence. It has been the first to show what man's activity can bring about. It has accomplished wonders far surpassing Egyptian pyramids, Roman aqueducts, and Gothic cathedrals; it has conducted expeditions that put in the shade all former Exoduses of nations and crusades.

The bourgeoisie cannot exist without constantly revolutionizing the instruments of production, and thereby the relations of production, and with them the whole relations of society. Conservation of the old modes of production in unaltered form, was, on the contrary, the first condition of existence for all earlier industrial classes. Constant revolutionizing of production, uninterrupted disturbance of all social conditions, everlasting uncertainty and agitation distinguish the bourgeois epoch from all earlier ones. All fixed, fast-frozen relations, with their train of ancient and venerable prejudices and opinions, are swept away, all new-formed ones become antiquated before they can ossify. All that is solid melts into air, all that is holy is profaned, and man is at last compelled to face with sober senses, his real conditions of life, and his relations with his kind.

The need of a constantly expanding market for its products chases the bourgeoisie over the whole surface of the globe. It must nestle everywhere, settle everywhere, establish connections everywhere.

The bourgeoisie has through its exploitation of the world-market given a cosmopolitan character to production and consumption in every country. To the great chagrin of Reactionists, it has drawn from under the feet of industry the national ground on which it stood. All old-established national industries have been destroyed or are daily being destroyed. They are dislodged by new industries, whose introduction becomes a life and death question for all civilized nations, by industries that no longer work up indigenous raw material, but raw material drawn from the remotest zones; industries whose products are consumed, not only at home, but in every quarter of the globe. In place of the old wants, satisfied by the productions of the country, we find new wants, requiring for their satisfaction the products of distant lands and climes. In place of the old local and national seclusion and self-sufficiency, we have intercourse in every direction, universal inter-dependence of nations. And as in material, so also in intellectual production. The intellectual creations of individual nations become common property. National one-sidedness and narrow-mindedness become more and more impossible, and from the numerous national and local literatures, there arises a world literature.

The bourgeoisie, by the rapid improvement of all instruments of production, by the immensely facilitated means of communication, draws all, even the most barbarian, nations into civilization. The cheap prices of its commodities are the heavy artillery with which it batters down all Chinese walls, with which it forces the barbarians' intensely obstinate hatred of foreigners to capitulate. It compels all nations, on pain of extinction, to adopt the bourgeois mode of production; it compels them to introduce what it calls civilization into their midst, i.e., to become bourgeois themselves. In one word, it creates a world after its own image.

The bourgeoisie has subjected the country to the rule of the towns. It has created enormous cities, has greatly increased the urban population as compared with the rural, and has thus rescued a considerable part of the population from the idiocy of rural life. Just as it has made the country dependent on the towns, so it has made barbarian and semi-barbarian countries dependent on the civilized ones, nations of peasants on nations of bourgeois, the East on the West.

__The bourgeoisie keeps more and more doing away with the scattered state of the population, of the means of production, and of property. It has agglomerated production, and has concentrated property in a few hands.__ The necessary consequence of this was political centralization. Independent, or but loosely connected provinces, with separate interests, laws, governments and systems of taxation, became lumped together into one nation, with one government, one code of laws, one national class-interest, one frontier and one customs-tariff. The bourgeoisie, during its rule of scarce one hundred years, has created more massive and more colossal productive forces than have all preceding generations together. Subjection of Nature's forces to man, machinery, application of chemistry to industry and agriculture, steam-navigation, railways, electric telegraphs, clearing of whole continents for cultivation, canalization of rivers, whole populations conjured out of the ground -- what earlier century had even a presentiment that such productive forces slumbered in the lap of social labor?

We see then: the means of production and of exchange, on whose foundation the bourgeoisie built itself up, were generated in feudal society. At a certain stage in the development of these means of production and of exchange, the conditions under which feudal society produced and exchanged, the feudal organization of agriculture and manufacturing industry, in one word, the *__feudal relations of property__* became no longer compatible with the already developed productive forces; they became so many fetters. They had to be burst asunder; they were ***burst asunder***.

Into their place stepped free competition, accompanied by a social and political constitution adapted to it, and by the economical and political sway of the bourgeois class.

A similar movement is going on before our own eyes. Modern bourgeois society with its relations of production, of exchange and of property, a society that has conjured up such gigantic means of production and of exchange, is like the sorcerer, who is no longer able to control the powers of the nether world whom he has called up by his spells. For many a decade past the history of industry and commerce is but the history of the revolt of modern productive forces against modern conditions of production, against the property relations that are the conditions for the existence of the bourgeoisie and of its rule. It is enough to mention the commercial crises that by their periodical return put on its trial, each time more threateningly, the existence of the entire bourgeois society. In these crises a great part not only of the existing products, but also of the previously created productive forces, are periodically destroyed. In these crises there breaks out an epidemic that, in all earlier epochs, would have seemed an absurdity -- the epidemic of over-production. Society suddenly finds itself put back into a state of momentary barbarism; it appears as if a famine, a universal war of devastation had cut off the supply of every means of subsistence; industry and commerce seem to be destroyed; and why? Because there is too much civilization, too much means of subsistence, too much industry, too much commerce. The productive forces at the disposal of society no longer tend to further the development of the conditions of bourgeois property; on the contrary, they have become too powerful for these conditions, by which they are fettered, and so soon as they overcome these fetters, they bring disorder into the whole of bourgeois society, endanger the existence of bourgeois property. The conditions of bourgeois society are too narrow to comprise the wealth created by them. And how does the bourgeoisie get over these crises? On the one hand enforced destruction of a mass of productive forces; on the other, by the conquest of new markets, and by the more thorough exploitation of the old ones. That is to say, by paving the way for more extensive and more destructive crises, and by diminishing the means whereby crises are prevented.

The weapons with which the bourgeoisie felled feudalism to the ground are now turned against the bourgeoisie itself.

But ***not only has the bourgeoisie forged the weapons that bring*** *death to itself; it has also called into existence the men who are to wield those weapons -- the modern working class -- the proletarians.*

In proportion as the bourgeoisie, i.e., capital, is developed, in the same proportion is the proletariat, the modern working class, developed -- a class of laborers, who live only so long as they find work, and who find work only so long as their labor increases capital. These laborers, who must sell themselves piece-meal, are a commodity, like every other article of commerce, and are consequently exposed to all the vicissitudes of competition, to all the fluctuations of the market.

Proletariat includes illegal immigrants, speech/English challenged, and others brought down.

Owing to the extensive use of machinery and to division of labor, the work of the proletarians has lost all individual character, and consequently, all charm for the workman. He becomes an appendage of the machine, and it is only the most simple, most monotonous, and most easily acquired knack, that is required of him. Hence, the cost of production of a workman is restricted, almost entirely, to the means of subsistence that he requires for his maintenance, and for the propagation of his race. But the price of a commodity, and therefore also of labor, is equal to its cost of production. In proportion therefore, as the repulsiveness of the work increases, the wage decreases. Nay more, in proportion as the use of machinery and division of labor increases, in the same proportion the burden of toil also increases, whether by prolongation of the working hours, by increase of the work exacted in a given time or by increased speed of the machinery, etc.

Modern industry has converted the little workshop of the patriarchal master into the great factory of the industrial capitalist. Masses of laborers, crowded into the factory, are organized like soldiers. As privates of the industrial army they are placed under the command of a perfect hierarchy of officers and sergeants. Not only are they slaves of the bourgeois class, and of the bourgeois State; they are daily and hourly enslaved by the machine, by the over-looker, and, above all, by the individual bourgeois manufacturer himself. The more openly this despotism proclaims gain to be its end and aim, the more petty, the more hateful and the more embittering it is.

The less the skill and exertion of strength implied in manual labor, in other words, the more modern industry becomes developed, the more is the labor of men superseded by that of women. Differences of age and sex have no longer any distinctive social validity for the working class. All re instruments of labor, more or less expensive to use, according to their age and sex.

No sooner is the exploitation of the laborer by the manufacturer, so far at an end, that he receives his wages in cash, than he is set upon by the other portions of the bourgeoisie, the landlord, the shopkeeper, the pawnbroker, etc.

The *lower strata of the middle class -- the small tradespeople, shopkeepers, retired tradesmen generally, the handicraftsmen and peasants -- all these sink gradually into the proletariat*, partly because their diminutive capital does not suffice for the scale on which Modern Industry is carried on, and is swamped in the competition with the large capitalists, partly because their specialized skill is rendered worthless by the new methods of production. Thus the *proletariat is recruited from all classes of the population.*

The proletariat goes through various stages of development. With its birth begins its struggle with the bourgeoisie. At first the contest is carried on by individual laborers, then by the workpeople of a factory, then by the operatives of one trade, in one locality, against the individual bourgeois who directly exploits them. They direct their attacks not against the bourgeois conditions of production, but against the instruments of production themselves; they destroy imported wares that compete with their labor, they smash to pieces machinery, they set factories ablaze, they seek to restore by force the vanished status of the workman of the Middle Ages.

At this stage the *laborers still form an incoherent mass scattered over the whole country,* and broken up by their mutual competition. If anywhere they unite to form more compact bodies, this is not yet the consequence of their own active union, but of the union of the bourgeoisie, which class, in order to attain its own political ends, is compelled to set the whole proletariat in motion, and is moreover yet, for a time, able to do so. *At this stage*, therefore, the *proletarians do not fight their enemies, but the enemies of their enemies,* the remnants of absolute monarchy, the landowners, the non-industrial bourgeois, the petty bourgeoisie. Thus the whole historical movement is concentrated in the hands of the bourgeoisie; every victory so obtained is a victory for the bourgeoisie.

But *with the development of industry the proletariat not only increases in number; it becomes concentrated in greater masses, its strength grows, and it feels that strength more.* The various interests and conditions of life within the ranks of the proletariat are more and more equalized, in proportion as machinery obliterates all distinctions of labor, and nearly everywhere reduces wages to the same low level. The growing competition among the bourgeois, and the resulting commercial crises, make the wages of the workers ever more fluctuating. The unceasing improvement of machinery, ever more rapidly developing, makes their livelihood more and more precarious; the collisions between individual workmen and individual bourgeois take more and more the character of collisions between two classes. Thereupon the *__workers begin to form combinations (Trades Unions__* [**Tool #1**]*__) against the bourgeois;__* they club together in order to keep up the rate of wages; they found permanent associations in order to make provision beforehand for these occasional revolts. Here and there the contest breaks out into riots.

Now and then the workers are victorious, but only for a time. The real fruit of their battles lies, not in the immediate result, but in the ever-expanding union of the workers. This union is helped on by the improved means of communication that are created by modern industry and that place the workers of different localities in contact with one another. It was just this contact that was needed to centralize the numerous local struggles, all of the same character, into one national struggle between classes. But every class struggle is a political struggle. And that union, to attain which the burghers of the Middle Ages, with their miserable highways, required centuries, the modern proletarians, thanks to railways, achieve in a few years.

This *__organization of the proletarians into a class, and consequently into a political party__* (**Strategy**), is continually being upset again by the competition between the workers themselves. But it ever rises up again, stronger, firmer, mightier. It *__compels legislative recognition__* of particular interests of the workers, by taking advantage of the divisions among the bourgeoisie itself. Thus the ten-hours' bill in England was carried.

Altogether collisions between the classes of the old society further, in many ways, the course of development of the proletariat. The bourgeoisie finds itself involved in a constant battle. At first with the aristocracy; later on, with those portions of the bourgeoisie itself, whose interests have become antagonistic to the progress of industry; at all times, with the bourgeoisie of foreign countries. In all these battles it sees itself compelled to appeal to the proletariat, to ask for its help, and thus, to drag it into the political arena. The bourgeoisie itself, therefore, supplies the proletariat with its own instruments of political and general education, in other words, it furnishes the proletariat with weapons for fighting the bourgeoisie.

Further, as we have already seen, entire sections of the ruling classes are, by the advance of industry, precipitated into the proletariat, or are at least threatened in their conditions of existence. These also supply the proletariat with fresh elements of enlightenment and progress.

Finally, in times when the class struggle nears the decisive hour, the process of dissolution going on within the ruling class, in fact within the whole range of society, assumes such a violent, glaring character, that a small section of the ruling class cuts itself adrift, and joins the revolutionary class, the class that holds the future in its hands. Just as, therefore, at an earlier period, a section of the nobility went over to the bourgeoisie, so now a portion of the bourgeoisie goes over to the proletariat, and in particular, a portion of the bourgeois ideologists, who have raised themselves to the level of comprehending theoretically the historical movement as a whole.

Of all the classes that stand face to face with the bourgeoisie today, the proletariat alone is a really revolutionary class. The other classes decay and finally disappear in the face of Modern Industry; the proletariat is its special and essential product. The *lower middle class*, the small manufacturer, the shopkeeper, the artisan, the peasant, all these fight against the bourgeoisie, to save from extinction their existence as fractions of the middle class. They are therefore *not revolutionary*, but *conservative*. Nay more, they are *reactionary*, for they *try to roll back the wheel of history*. If by chance they are revolutionary, they are so only in view of their impending transfer into the proletariat, they thus defend not their present, but their future interests, they desert their own standpoint to place themselves at that of the proletariat.

The *"dangerous class," the social scum,* that passively rotting mass thrown off by the lowest layers of old society, may, here and there, be swept into the movement by a proletarian revolution; its conditions of life, however, prepare it far more for the part of a bribed tool of reactionary intrigue.

In the conditions of the proletariat, those of old society at large are already virtually swamped. The *proletarian is without property; his relation to his wife and children has no longer anything in common with the bourgeois family-relations;* modern industrial labor, modern subjection to capital, the same in England as in France, in America as in Germany, has *stripped him of every trace of national character. Law, morality, religion, are to him so many bourgeois prejudices,* behind which lurk in ambush just as many bourgeois interests.

All the preceding classes that got the upper hand, sought to fortify their already acquired status by subjecting society at large to their conditions of appropriation. The proletarians cannot become masters of the productive forces of society, except by abolishing their own previous mode of appropriation, and thereby also every other previous mode of appropriation. _**They have nothing of their own to secure and to fortify; their mission is to destroy all previous securities for, and insurances of, individual property.**_

All _**previous historical movements**_ were _**movements of minorities**_, or in the interests of minorities. The _**proletarian movement is the self-conscious, independent movement of the immense majority, in the interests of the immense majority. The proletariat, the lowest stratum of our present society, cannot stir, cannot raise itself up, without the whole superincumbent strata of official society being sprung into the air.**_

Though not in substance, yet in form, the struggle of the proletariat with the bourgeoisie is _**at first a national struggle**_. The proletariat of each country must, of course, first of all settle matters with its own bourgeoisie.

In depicting the most general phases of the development of the proletariat, we traced the more or less veiled civil war, raging within existing society, up to the point where that war breaks out into open revolution, and where the _**violent overthrow of the bourgeoisie lays the foundation for the sway of the proletariat.**_

Hitherto, every form of society has been based, as we have already seen, on the antagonism of oppressing and oppressed classes. But in order to oppress a class, certain conditions must be assured to it under which it can, at least, continue its slavish existence. The serf, in the period of serfdom, raised himself to membership in the commune, just as the petty bourgeois, under the yoke of feudal absolutism, managed to develop into a bourgeois. The _**modern laborer,**_ on the contrary, instead of rising with the progress of industry, sinks deeper and deeper below the conditions of existence of his own class. He _**becomes a pauper**_ (**Critical Objective**), and pauperism develops more rapidly than population and wealth. And here it becomes evident, that the _**bourgeoisie is unfit any longer to be the ruling class in society,**_ and to impose its conditions of existence upon society as an over-riding law. _**It is unfit to rule because it is incompetent to assure an existence to its slave within his slavery, because it cannot help letting him sink into such a state, that it has to feed him, instead**_ *of being fed by him.* Society can no longer live under this bourgeoisie, in other words, its existence is no longer compatible with society.

The *__essential condition for the existence, and for the sway of the bourgeois class, is the formation and augmentation of capital__* (**Destruction of Capital = Destruction of Bourgeoisie**); the condition for capital is wage-labor. Wage-labor rests exclusively on competition between the laborers. The advance of industry, whose involuntary promoter is the bourgeoisie, replaces the isolation of the laborers, due to competition, by their revolutionary combination, due to association. The development of Modern Industry, therefore, cuts from under its feet the very foundation on which the bourgeoisie produces and appropriates products. *__What the bourgeoisie, therefore, produces, above all, is its own grave-diggers. Its fall and the victory of the proletariat are equally inevitable.__*

Section II. Proletarians and Communists

In *__what relation do the Communists stand to the proletarians as a whole__*?

The Communists do not form a separate party opposed to other working-class parties.

They have *__no interests separate and apart from those of the proletariat__* as a whole.

They do not set up any sectarian principles of their own, by which to shape and mould the proletarian movement.

The Communists are distinguished from the other working-class parties by this only:

(1) In the national struggles of the proletarians of the different countries, they *__point out and bring to the front the common interests of the entire proletariat, independently of all nationality.__*

(2) In the various stages of development which the struggle of the working class against the bourgeoisie has to pass through, *__they always and everywhere represent the interests of the movement as a whole.__*

The Communists, therefore, are on the one hand, practically, the *__most advanced and resolute section of the working-class parties of every country,__* that section which pushes forward all others; on the other hand, theoretically, they have over the great mass of the proletariat the *__advantage of clearly understanding the line of march, the conditions, and the ultimate general results of the proletarian movement.__*

The *__immediate aim of the Communist__* is the same as that of all the other proletarian parties: *__formation of the proletariat into a class,__* *overthrow of the bourgeois supremacy, conquest of political power by the proletariat.*

The theoretical conclusions of the Communists are in no way based on ideas or principles that have been invented, or discovered, by this or that would-be universal reformer. They merely express, in general terms, actual relations springing from an existing class struggle, from a historical movement going on under our very eyes. The abolition of existing property relations is not at all a distinctive feature of Communism.

All property relations in the past have continually been subject to historical change consequent upon the change in historical conditions.

The French Revolution, for example, abolished feudal property in favor of bourgeois property.

The distinguishing feature of Communism is not the abolition of property generally, but the ***abolition of bourgeois property.*** But modern bourgeois private property is the final and most complete expression of the system of producing and appropriating products, that is based on class antagonisms, on the exploitation of the many by the few.

In this sense, ***the theory of the Communists*** may be ***summed up*** in the single sentence: ***Abolition of private property.*** (**Desired End Result**)

We Communists have been reproached with the desire of abolishing the right of personally acquiring property as the fruit of a man's own labor, which property is alleged to be the groundwork of all personal freedom, activity and independence.

Hard-won, self-acquired, self-earned property! Do you mean the property of the petty artisan and of the small peasant, a form of property that preceded the bourgeois form? There is no need to abolish that; the development of industry has to a great extent already destroyed it, and is still destroying it daily.

Or do you mean modern bourgeois private property?

But ***does wage-labor create any property for the laborer? Not a bit. It creates capital,*** i.e., that kind of property which exploits wage-labor, and which cannot increase except upon condition of begetting a new supply of wage-labor for fresh exploitation. Property, in its present form, is based on the antagonism of capital and wage-labor. Let us examine both sides of this antagonism.

To be a capitalist, is to have not only a purely personal, but a social status in production. Capital is a collective product, and only by the united action of many members, nay, in the last resort, only by the united action of all members of society, can it be set in motion.

Capital is, therefore, not a personal, it is *a social power*.

When, therefore, *capital is converted into common property, into the property of all members of society, personal property is not* thereby transformed into social property. It is only the social character of the property that is changed. It loses its class-character.

Let us now take wage-labor.

The *average price of wage-labor is the minimum wage*, i.e., that quantum of the means of subsistence, which is absolutely requisite in bare existence as a laborer. What, therefore, the wage-laborer appropriates by means of his labor, merely suffices to prolong and reproduce a bare existence. *We by no means intend to abolish this personal appropriation of the products of labor, an appropriation that is made for the maintenance and reproduction of human life,* and that leaves no surplus wherewith to command the labor of others. All that *we want to do away with, is the miserable character of this appropriation,* under which the laborer lives merely to increase capital, and is allowed to live only in so far as the interest of the ruling class requires it.

In bourgeois society, living labor is but a means to increase accumulated labor. In Communist society, accumulated labor is but a means to widen, to enrich, to promote the existence of the laborer.

In *bourgeois society,* therefore, the *past dominates the present;* in *Communist society,* the *present dominates the past* **(a critically important concept when planning educational curriculum. In the 1970's, U.S. public schools replaced history and like courses with Social Studies [AKA Socialism], resulting in "historically illiterate" students and graduates).** In bourgeois society capital is independent and has individuality, while the living person is dependent and has no individuality.

And the abolition of this state of things is called by the bourgeois, abolition of individuality and freedom! And rightly so. The *abolition of bourgeois individuality, bourgeois independence, and bourgeois freedom is undoubtedly aimed at.*

By freedom is meant, under the present bourgeois conditions of production, free trade, free selling and buying.

But if selling and buying disappears, free selling and buying disappears also. This talk about free selling and buying, and all the other "brave words" of our bourgeoisie about freedom in general, have a meaning, if any, only in contrast with restricted selling and buying, with the fettered traders of the Middle Ages, but have no meaning when opposed to the Communistic abolition of buying and selling, of the bourgeois conditions of production, and of the bourgeoisie itself.

You are horrified at our intending to do away with private property. But in your existing society, private property is already done away with for nine-tenths of the population; its existence for the few is solely due to its non-existence in the hands of those nine-tenths. You reproach us, therefore, with intending to do away with a form of property, the necessary condition for whose existence is the non-existence of any property for the immense majority of society.

In one word, you reproach us with intending to do away with your property. Precisely so; that is just what we intend.

From the moment when labor can no longer be converted into capital, money, or rent, into a social power capable of being monopolized, i.e., from the moment when individual property can no longer be transformed into bourgeois property, into capital, from that moment, you say individuality vanishes.

You must, therefore, confess that by *"**individual**"* you mean no other person than the bourgeois, than ***the middle-class owner of property. This person must, indeed, be swept out of the way, and made impossible.***

Communism deprives no man of the power to appropriate the products of society; all that it does is to deprive him of the power to subjugate the labor of others by means of such appropriation.

It has been objected that upon the abolition of private property all work will cease, and universal laziness will overtake us.

According to this, ***bourgeois society ought long ago to have gone to the dogs through sheer idleness;*** for those of its members who work, acquire nothing, and ***those who acquire anything, do not work.*** The whole of this objection is but another expression of the tautology: that there can no longer be any wage-labor when there is no longer any capital.

All objections urged against the Communistic mode of producing and appropriating material products, have, in the same way, been urged against the Communistic modes of producing and appropriating intellectual products. Just as, to the bourgeois, the disappearance of class property is the disappearance of production itself, so the disappearance of class culture is to him identical with the disappearance of all culture.

That ***culture***, the loss of which he laments, is, for the enormous majority, a ***mere training to act as a machine.***

33

But don't wrangle with us so long as you apply, to our intended abolition of bourgeois property, the standard of your bourgeois notions of freedom, culture, law, etc. Your very ideas are but the outgrowth of the conditions of your bourgeois production and bourgeois property, just as your jurisprudence is but the will of your class made into a law for all, a will, whose essential character and direction are determined by the economical conditions of existence of your class.

The selfish misconception that induces you to transform into eternal laws of nature and of reason, the social forms springing from your present mode of production and form of property -- historical relations that rise and disappear in the progress of production -- this misconception you share with every ruling class that has preceded you. What you see clearly in the case of ancient property, what you admit in the case of feudal property, you are of course forbidden to admit in the case of your own bourgeois form of property.

**Abolition of the family!** Even the most radical flare up at this infamous proposal of the Communists.

On what foundation is the present family, the bourgeois family, based? On capital, on private gain. In its completely developed form this family exists only among the bourgeoisie. But this state of things finds its complement in the practical absence of the family among the proletarians, and in public prostitution **(since 1960's, state and federal laws passed that facilitated divorce [AKA no fault divorce] and supported single parenthood).**

The bourgeois family will vanish as a matter of course when its complement vanishes, and both will vanish with the vanishing of capital.

Do you charge us with wanting to _**stop the exploitation of children by their parents**_? To this crime we plead guilty.

But, you will say, we destroy the most hallowed of relations, when we _**replace home education by social.**_

And your education! Is not that also social, and determined by the social conditions under which you educate, by the intervention, direct or indirect, of society, by means of schools, etc.? The _**Communists**_ have not invented the intervention of society in education; they do but seek to alter the character of that intervention, and to _**rescue education from the influence of the ruling class.**_ **(In 1935, Columbia University in New York City welcomed dissident Marxist scholars from the "Frankfurt School" into their faculty. They were fleeing the University of Frankfurt because of Hitler's rise in power and the growing**

influence in Germany of "National" Socialism. The ramifications of their teachings now extend to all of U.S. academia).

The bourgeois clap-trap about the family and education, about the hallowed co-relation of parent and child, becomes all the more disgusting, the more, by the action of Modern Industry, *__all family ties among the proletarians are torn asunder__*, and their children transformed into simple articles of commerce and instruments of labor.

But you Communists would introduce community of women, screams the whole bourgeoisie in chorus.

The bourgeois sees in his wife a mere instrument of production. He hears that the instruments of production are to be exploited in common, and, naturally, can come to no other conclusion than that the lot of being common to all will likewise fall to the women.

He has not even a suspicion that the *__real point is to do away with the status of women as mere instruments of production__* **(in 1973 the US Supreme Court decision on Roe v. Wade incorporated recommendations for easy access to abortion, subsequently the use of abortion for birth control and the push for premarital sex [AKA sexual revolution] rose).**

For the rest, nothing is more ridiculous than the virtuous indignation of our bourgeois at the community of women which, they pretend, is to be openly and officially established by the Communists. The Communists have no need to introduce community of women; it has existed almost from time immemorial.

Our bourgeois, not content with having the wives and daughters of their proletarians at their disposal, not to speak of common prostitutes, take the greatest pleasure in seducing each other's wives.

Bourgeois marriage is in reality a system of wives in common and thus, at the most, what the Communists might possibly be reproached with, is that they desire to introduce, in substitution for a hypocritically concealed, an openly legalized community of women. For the rest, it is self-evident that the abolition of the present system of production must bring with it the abolition of the community of women springing from that system, i.e., of prostitution both public and private.

The *__Communists are further reproached with desiring to abolish countries and nationality.__*

No Country = No Nation = No Borders

The *__working men have no country__*. We cannot take from them what they have not got. Since the *__proletariat must first of all acquire political__* _**supremacy,**_ must rise to be the leading class of the nation, must constitute itself the nation, it is, so far, itself national, though not in the bourgeois sense of the word.

National differences and antagonisms between peoples are daily more and more vanishing, owing to the development of the bourgeoisie, to freedom of commerce, to the world-market, to uniformity in the mode of production and in the conditions of life corresponding thereto.

The supremacy of the proletariat will cause them to vanish still faster. _**United action, of the leading civilized countries at least, is one of the first conditions for the emancipation of the proletariat.**_

In proportion as the exploitation of one individual by another is put an end to, the exploitation of one nation by another will also be put an end to. In proportion as the antagonism between classes within the nation vanishes, the hostility of one nation to another will come to an end.

The _**charges against Communism made from a religious, a philosophical, and, generally, from an ideological standpoint, are not deserving of serious examination.**_

Does it require deep intuition to comprehend that man's ideas, views and conceptions, in one word, man's consciousness, changes with every change in the conditions of his material existence, in his social relations and in his social life?

What else does the history of ideas prove, than that intellectual production changes its character in proportion as material production is changed? The ruling ideas of each age have ever been the ideas of its ruling class.

When people speak of ideas that revolutionize society, they do but express the fact, that within the old society, the elements of a new one have been created, and that the dissolution of the old ideas keeps even pace with the dissolution of the old conditions of existence.

When the ancient world was in its last throes, the ancient religions were overcome by Christianity. When Christian ideas succumbed in the 18th century to rationalist ideas, feudal society fought its death battle with the then revolutionary bourgeoisie. The ideas of religious liberty and freedom of conscience merely gave expression to the sway of free competition within the domain of knowledge.

"Undoubtedly," it will be said, "religious, moral, philosophical, and juridical ideas have been modified in the course of historical development. But religion, morality, philosophy, political science, and law constantly survived this change."

"There are, besides, eternal truths, such as Freedom, Justice, etc. that are common to all states of society. *__But Communism abolishes eternal truths, it abolishes all religion, and all morality,__* (**Critically important -- most Communists are atheists**), instead of constituting them on a new basis; it therefore acts in contradiction to all past historical experience."

What does this accusation reduce itself to? The *__history__* of all past society has consisted in the development of *__class antagonisms__*, antagonisms that assumed different forms at different epochs.

But whatever form they may have taken, one fact is common to all past ages, viz., the *__exploitation of one part of society by the other.__* No wonder, then, that the social consciousness of past ages, despite all the multiplicity and variety it displays, moves within certain common forms, or general ideas, which cannot completely vanish except with the total disappearance of class antagonisms.

The Communist revolution is the most radical rupture with traditional property relations; no wonder that its development involves the most radical rupture with traditional ideas.

But let us have done with the bourgeois objections to Communism.

We have seen above, that the *__first step in the revolution by the working class, is to raise the proletariat to the position of ruling as to win the battle of democracy.__*

The *__proletariat will use its political supremacy to wrest, by degrees, all capital from the bourgeoisie, to centralize all instruments of production in the hands of the State, i.e., of the proletariat organized as the ruling class; and to increase the total of productive forces as rapidly as possible.__* (**Critically important**)

Of course, in the beginning, this cannot be effected except by means of despotic inroads on the rights of property, and on the conditions of bourgeois production; by means of measures, therefore, which appear economically insufficient and untenable, but which, in the course of the movement, outstrip themselves, necessitate further inroads upon the old social order, and are unavoidable as a means of entirely *__revolutionizing__* the mode of production.

These measures will of course be different in different countries.

Nevertheless *__in the most advanced countries, the following will be pretty generally applicable.__*

__1.__ Abolition of property in land and application of all rents of land to public purposes.

(the Supreme Court decided in 2005, Kelo v. City of New

London, 545 U.S. 469, that eminent domain power, that is the government seizure of and payment for private land without the consent of the owner, could be used not only for public purposes like roads and schools but also to increase municipal revenues)

2. A heavy progressive or graduated income tax.

(16th Amendment to the Constitution of the United States, added in 1913, a confiscatory [not a consumption] tax)

3. Abolition of all right of inheritance.

4. Confiscation of the property of all emigrants and rebels.

5. Centralization of credit in the hands of the State, by means of a national bank with State capital and an exclusive monopoly.

6. Centralization of the means of communication and transport in the hands of the State.

7. Extension of factories and instruments of production owned by the State; the bringing into cultivation of waste-lands, and the improvement of the soil generally in accordance with a common plan.

8. Equal liability of all to labor. Establishment of industrial armies, especially for agriculture.

9. Combination of agriculture with manufacturing industries; gradual abolition of the distinction between town and country, by a more equable distribution of the population over the country.

10. Free education for all children in public schools. Abolition of children's factory labor in its present form. Combination of education with industrial production, &c., &c.

(For indoctrination or dumbing down)

When, in the course of development, class distinctions have disappeared, and *all production has been concentrated in the hands of a vast association of the whole nation, the public power will lose its political character.* Political power, properly so called, is merely the *organized power of one class for oppressing another.* If the proletariat during its contest with the bourgeoisie is compelled, by the force of circumstances, to organize itself as a class, if, by means of a revolution, it makes itself the ruling class, and, as such, sweeps away by force the old conditions of production, then it will, along with these conditions, have swept away the conditions for the existence of class antagonisms and of classes generally, and will thereby have abolished its own supremacy as a class.

In place of the old bourgeois society, with its classes and class

antagonisms, we shall have ***an association***, in which the ***free development of each is the condition for the free development of all***.
     (But <u>NO</u> incentive for the individual)

Section III. Socialist and Communist Literature

1. REACTIONARY SOCIALISM

A. Feudal Socialism

Owing to their historical position, it became the vocation of the aristocracies of France and England to write pamphlets against modern bourgeois society. In the French revolution of July 1830, and in the English reform agitation, these aristocracies again succumbed to the hateful upstart. Thenceforth, a serious political contest was altogether out of the question. A literary battle alone remained possible. But even in the domain of literature the old cries of the restoration period had become impossible.

In order to arouse sympathy, the aristocracy were obliged to lose sight, apparently, of their own interests, and to formulate their indictment against the bourgeoisie in the interest of the exploited working class alone. Thus the aristocracy took their revenge by singing lampoons on their new master, and whispering in his ears sinister prophecies of coming catastrophe.

In this way arose ***Feudal Socialism***: half lamentation, half lampoon; half echo of the past, half menace of the future; at times, by its bitter, witty and incisive criticism, striking the bourgeoisie to the very heart's core; but ***always ludicrous*** in its effect, through total incapacity to comprehend the march of modern history.

The aristocracy, in order to rally the people to them, waved the proletarian alms-bag in front for a banner. But the people, so often as it joined them, saw on their hindquarters the old feudal coats of arms, and deserted with loud and irreverent laughter.

One section of the French Legitimists and "Young England" exhibited this spectacle.

In pointing out that their mode of exploitation was different to that of the bourgeoisie, the feudalists forget that they exploited under circumstances and conditions that were quite different, and that are now antiquated. In showing that, under their rule, the modern proletariat never existed, they forget that the modern bourgeoisie is the necessary offspring of their own form of society.

For the rest, so little do they conceal the reactionary character of their criticism that their chief accusation against the bourgeoisie amounts to this, that under the bourgeois regime a class is being developed, which is destined to cut up root and branch the old order of society.

What they upbraid the bourgeoisie with is not so much that it creates a proletariat, as that it creates a revolutionary proletariat.

In political practice, therefore, they join in all coercive measures against the working class; and in ordinary life, despite their high falutin phrases, they stoop to pick up the golden apples dropped from the tree of industry, and to barter truth, love, and honor for traffic in wool, beetroot-sugar, and potato spirits.

As the parson has ever gone band in hand with the landlord, so has Clerical Socialism with Feudal Socialism.

Nothing is easier than to give Christian asceticism a Socialist tinge. Has not Christianity declaimed against private property, against marriage, against the State? Has it not preached in the place of these, charity and poverty, celibacy and mortification of the flesh, monastic life and Mother Church? Christian Socialism is but the holy water with which the priest consecrates the heart-burnings of the aristocrat.

B. Petty-Bourgeois Socialism

The feudal aristocracy was not the only class that was ruined by the bourgeoisie, not the only class whose conditions of existence pined and perished in the atmosphere of modern bourgeois society. The mediaeval burgesses and the small peasant proprietors were the precursors of the modern bourgeoisie. In those countries which are but little developed, industrially and commercially, these two classes still vegetate side by side with the rising bourgeoisie.

In countries where modern civilization has become fully developed, a new class of petty bourgeois has been formed, fluctuating between proletariat and bourgeoisie and ever renewing itself as a supplementary part of bourgeois society. The individual members of this class, however, are being constantly hurled down into the proletariat by the action of competition, and, as modern industry develops, they even see the moment approaching when they will completely disappear as an independent section of modern society, to be replaced, in manufactures, agriculture and commerce, by overlookers, bailiffs and shopmen.

In countries like France, where the peasants constitute far more than half of the population, it was natural that writers who sided with the proletariat against the bourgeoisie, should use, in their criticism of the bourgeois regime, the standard of the peasant and petty bourgeois, and from the standpoint of these intermediate classes should take up the cudgels for the working class. Thus arose petty-bourgeois Socialism. Sismondi was the head of this school, not only in France but also in England.

This school of Socialism dissected with great acuteness the contradictions in the conditions of modern production. It laid bare the hypocritical apologies of economists. It proved, incontrovertibly, the disastrous effects of machinery and division of labor; the concentration of capital and land in a few hands; overproduction and crises; it pointed out the inevitable ruin of the petty bourgeois and peasant, the misery of the proletariat, the anarchy in production, the crying inequalities in the distribution of wealth, the industrial war of extermination between nations, the dissolution of old moral bonds, of the old family relations, of the old nationalities.

In its positive aims, however, this form of Socialism aspires either to restoring the old means of production and of exchange, and with them the old property relations, and the old society, or to cramping the modern means of production and of exchange, within the framework of the old property relations that have been, and were bound to be, exploded by those means. In either case, it is both ***reactionary and Utopian***.

Its last words are: corporate guilds for manufacture, patriarchal relations in agriculture.

Ultimately, when stubborn historical facts had dispersed all intoxicating effects of self-deception, ***this form of Socialism ended in a miserable fit of the blues.***

C. German, or "True," Socialism

The Socialist and Communist literature of France, a literature that originated under the pressure of a bourgeoisie in power, and that was the expression of the struggle against this power, was introduced into Germany at a time when the bourgeoisie, in that country, had just begun its contest with feudal absolutism.

German philosophers, would-be philosophers, and beaux esprits, eagerly seized on this literature, only forgetting, that when these writings immigrated from France into Germany, French social conditions had not immigrated along with them. In contact with German social conditions, this French literature lost all its immediate practical significance, and assumed a purely literary aspect. Thus, to the German philosophers of the eighteenth century, the demands of the first French Revolution were nothing more than the demands of "Practical Reason" in general, and the utterance of the will of the revolutionary French bourgeoisie signified in their eyes the law of pure Will, of Will as it was bound to be, of true human Will generally.

The world of the German literate consisted solely in bringing the new French ideas into harmony with their ancient philosophical conscience, or rather, in annexing the French ideas without deserting their own philosophic point of view.

This annexation took place in the same way in which a foreign language is appropriated, namely, by translation.

It is well known how the monks wrote silly lives of Catholic Saints over the manuscripts on which the classical works of ancient heathendom had been written. The German literate reversed this process with the profane French literature. They wrote their philosophical nonsense beneath the French original. For instance, beneath the French criticism of the economic functions of money, they wrote "Alienation of Humanity," and beneath the French criticism of the bourgeois State they wrote "dethronement of the Category of the General," and so forth.

The introduction of these philosophical phrases at the back of the French historical criticisms they dubbed "Philosophy of Action," "True Socialism," "German Science of Socialism," "Philosophical Foundation of Socialism," and so on.

The French Socialist and Communist literature was thus completely emasculated. And, since it ceased in the hands of the German to express the struggle of one class with the other, he felt conscious of having overcome "French one-sidedness" and of representing, not true requirements, but the requirements of truth; not the interests of the proletariat, but the interests of Human Nature, of Man in general, who belongs to no class, has no reality, who exists only in the misty realm of philosophical fantasy.

This German Socialism, which took its schoolboy task so seriously and solemnly, and extolled its poor stock-in-trade in such mountebank fashion, meanwhile gradually lost its pedantic innocence.

The fight of the German, and especially, of the Prussian bourgeoisie, against feudal aristocracy and absolute monarchy, in other words, the *liberal movement* (**now known as progressive**), became more earnest.

By this, the long wished-for opportunity was offered to "True" Socialism of confronting the political movement with the Socialist demands, of hurling the traditional anathemas against liberalism, against representative government, against bourgeois competition, bourgeois freedom of the press, bourgeois legislation, bourgeois liberty and equality, and of preaching to the masses that they had nothing to gain, and everything to lose, by this bourgeois movement. ***German Socialism forgot, in the nick of time, that the French criticism, whose silly echo it was, presupposed the existence of modern bourgeois society, with its corresponding economic conditions of existence, and the political constitution adapted thereto, the very things whose attainment was the object of the pending struggle in Germany.***

To the absolute governments, with their following of parsons, professors, country squires and officials, it served as a welcome scarecrow against the threatening bourgeoisie.

It was a sweet finish after the bitter pills of floggings and bullets with which these same governments, just at that time, dosed the German working-class risings.

While this "True" Socialism thus served the governments as a weapon for fighting the German bourgeoisie, it, at the same time, directly represented a reactionary interest, the interest of the German Philistines. In Germany the petty-bourgeois class, a relic of the sixteenth century, and since then constantly cropping up again under various forms, is the real social basis of the existing state of things.

To preserve this class is to preserve the existing state of things in Germany. The industrial and political supremacy of the bourgeoisie threatens it with certain destruction; on the one hand, from the concentration of capital; on the other, from the rise of a revolutionary proletariat. "True" Socialism appeared to kill these two birds with one stone. It spread like an epidemic.

The robe of speculative cobwebs, embroidered with flowers of rhetoric, steeped in the dew of sickly sentiment, this transcendental robe in which the German Socialists wrapped their sorry "eternal truths," all skin and bone, served to wonderfully increase the sale of their goods amongst such a public. And on its part, German Socialism recognized, more and more, its own calling as the bombastic representative of the petty- bourgeois Philistine.

It proclaimed the German nation to be the model nation, and the German petty Philistine to be the typical man. To every villainous meanness of this model man it gave a hidden, higher, Socialistic interpretation, the exact contrary of its real character. ***It went to the extreme length of directly*** *opposing the "brutally destructive" tendency of Communism*, and of proclaiming its supreme and impartial contempt of all class struggles. With very few exceptions, all the so-called Socialist and Communist publications that now (1847) circulate in Germany belong to the domain of this foul and enervating literature.

2. CONSERVATIVE, OR BOURGEOIS, SOCIALISM

A part of the bourgeoisie is desirous of redressing social grievances, in order to secure the continued existence of bourgeois society.

To this section belong *economists, philanthropists, humanitarians, improvers of the condition of the working class, organizers of charity, members of societies for the prevention of cruelty to animals, temperance fanatics, hole-and-corner reformers of every imaginable kind.* This form of Socialism has, moreover, been worked out into complete systems.

We may cite Proudhon's Philosophie de la Misere as an example of this form.

The Socialistic bourgeois want all the advantages of modern social conditions without the struggles and dangers necessarily resulting therefrom. They desire the existing state of society minus its revolutionary and disintegrating elements. They wish for a bourgeoisie without a proletariat. The bourgeoisie naturally conceives the world in which it is supreme to be the best; and bourgeois Socialism develops this comfortable conception into various more or less complete systems. In requiring the proletariat to carry out such a system, and thereby to march straightway into the social New Jerusalem, it but requires in reality, that the proletariat should remain within the bounds of existing society, but should cast away all its hateful ideas concerning the bourgeoisie.

A second and more practical, but less systematic, form of this Socialism sought to depreciate every revolutionary movement in the eyes of the working class, by showing that no mere political reform, but only a change in the material conditions of existence, in economic relations, could be of any advantage to them. By changes in the material conditions of existence, this form of Socialism, however, by no means understands abolition of the bourgeois relations of production, an abolition that can be effected only by a revolution, but administrative reforms, based on the continued existence of these relations; reforms, therefore, that in no respect affect the relations between capital and labor, but, at the best, lessen the cost, and simplify the administrative work, of bourgeois government.

Bourgeois Socialism attains adequate expression, when, and only when, it becomes a mere figure of speech.

Free trade: for the benefit of the working class. Protective duties: for the benefit of the working class. Prison Reform: for the benefit of the working class. This is the last word and the only seriously meant word of bourgeois Socialism.

It is summed up in the phrase: the *bourgeois is a bourgeois -- for the benefit of the working class.*

3. *CRITICAL-UTOPIAN SOCIALISM AND COMMUNISM*

We do not here refer to that literature which, in every great modern revolution, has always given voice to the demands of the proletariat, such as the writings of Babeuf and others.

The first direct attempts of the proletariat to attain its own ends, made in times of universal excitement, when feudal society was being overthrown, these attempts necessarily failed, owing to the then undeveloped state of the proletariat, as well as to the absence of the economic conditions for its emancipation, conditions that had yet to be produced, and could be produced by the impending bourgeois epoch alone. The revolutionary literature that accompanied these first movements of the proletariat had necessarily a reactionary character. It inculcated universal asceticism and social leveling in its crudest form.

The Socialist and Communist systems properly so called, those of Saint-Simon, Fourier, Owen and others, spring into existence in the early undeveloped period, described above, of the struggle between proletariat and bourgeoisie (see Section 1. Bourgeois and Proletarians).

The founders of these systems see, indeed, the class antagonisms, as well as the action of the decomposing elements, in the prevailing form of society. But the *proletariat, as yet in its infancy, offers to them the spectacle of a class without any historical initiative or any independent political movement*.

Since the development of class antagonism keeps even pace with the development of industry, the economic situation, as they find it, does not as yet offer to them the material conditions for the emancipation of the proletariat. They therefore search after a new social science, after new social laws, that are to create these conditions.

Historical action is to yield to their personal inventive action, historically created conditions of emancipation to fantastic ones, and the gradual, spontaneous class-organization of the proletariat to the organization of society specially contrived by these inventors. Future history resolves itself, in their eyes, into the propaganda and the practical carrying out of their social plans.

In the formation of their plans they are conscious of caring chiefly for the interests of the working class, as being the most suffering class. ***Only from the point of view of being the most suffering class does the proletariat exist for them.***

The undeveloped state of the class struggle, as well as their own surroundings, causes Socialists of this kind to consider themselves far superior to all class antagonisms. They want to improve the condition of every member of society, even that of the most favored. Hence, they habitually appeal to society at large, without distinction of class; nay, by preference, to the ruling class. For how can people, when once they understand their system, fail to see in it the best possible plan of the best possible state of society?

Hence, they reject all political, and especially all revolutionary, action; they wish to attain their ends by peaceful means, and endeavor, by small experiments, necessarily doomed to failure, and by the force of example, to pave the way for the new social Gospel.

Such fantastic pictures of future society, painted at a time when the proletariat is still in a very undeveloped state and has but a fantastic conception of its own position correspond with the first instinctive yearnings of that class for a general reconstruction of society.

But these Socialist and Communist publications contain also a critical element. They attack every principle of existing society. Hence they are full of the most valuable materials for the enlightenment of the working class. The practical measures proposed in them -- such as the abolition of the distinction between town and country, of the family, of the carrying on of industries for the account of private individuals, and of the wage system, the proclamation of social harmony, the conversion of the functions of the State into a mere superintendence of production, all these proposals, point solely to the disappearance of class antagonisms which were, at that time, only just cropping up, and which, in these publications, are recognized in their earliest, indistinct and undefined forms only. These ***proposals***, therefore, ***are of a purely Utopian character.***

The significance of Critical-Utopian Socialism and Communism bears an inverse relation to historical development. In proportion as the modern class struggle develops and takes definite shape, this fantastic standing apart from the contest, these fantastic attacks on it, lose all practical value and all theoretical justification. Therefore, although the ***originators of these systems were, in many respects, revolutionary, their disciples have, in every case, formed mere reactionary sects.*** They hold fast by the original views of their masters, in opposition to the progressive historical development of the proletariat. They, therefore, ***endeavor,*** and that consistently, ***to deaden the class struggle and to reconcile the class antagonisms.*** They still dream of experimental realization of their social Utopias, of founding isolated "phalansteres," of establishing "Home Colonies," of setting up a "Little Icaria" -- duodecimo editions of the New Jerusalem -- and to realize all these castles in the air, they are compelled to appeal to the feelings and purses of the bourgeois. ***By degrees they sink into the category of the reactionary conservative Socialists depicted above***, differing from these only by more systematic pedantry, and by their fanatical and superstitious belief in the miraculous effects of their social science.

They, therefore, violently oppose all political action on the part of the working class; such action, according to them, can only result from blind unbelief in the new Gospel.

The Owenites in England, and the Fourierists in France, respectively, oppose the Chartists and the Reformists.

Major Tools and/or Agents for Communists:
#1 Trade Unions
#2 Socialists

Section IV. Position of the Communists in Relation to the Various Existing Opposition Parties

Section II has made clear the relations of the Communists to the existing working-class parties, such as the Chartists in England and the Agrarian Reformers in America.

The Communists fight for the attainment of the immediate aims, for the enforcement of the momentary interests of the working class; but in the movement of the present, they also represent and take care of the future of that movement. In France the Communists ally themselves with the Social-Democrats, against the conservative and radical bourgeoisie, reserving, however, the right to take up a critical position in regard to phrases and illusions traditionally handed down from the great Revolution.

In Switzerland they support the Radicals, without losing sight of the fact that this party consists of antagonistic elements, partly of Democratic Socialists, in the French sense, partly of radical bourgeois.

In Poland they support the party that insists on an agrarian revolution as the prime condition for national emancipation, that party which fomented the insurrection of Cracow in 1846.

In Germany they fight with the bourgeoisie whenever it acts in a revolutionary way, against the absolute monarchy, the feudal squirearchy, and the petty bourgeoisie.

But they never cease, for a single instant, to instill into the working class the clearest possible recognition of the hostile antagonism between bourgeoisie and proletariat, in order that the German workers may straightaway use, as so many weapons against the bourgeoisie, the social and political conditions that the bourgeoisie must necessarily introduce along with its supremacy, and in order that, after the fall of the reactionary classes in Germany, the fight against the bourgeoisie itself may immediately begin.

The Communists turn their attention chiefly to Germany, because that country is on the eve of a bourgeois revolution that is bound to be carried out under more advanced conditions of European civilization, and with a much more developed proletariat, than that of England was in the seventeenth, and of France in the eighteenth century, and because the bourgeois revolution in Germany will be but the prelude to an immediately following proletarian revolution.

In short, the Communists everywhere support every revolutionary movement against the existing social and political order of things. **(layman's definition of a Communist: A Socialist with a gun [original source unknown])**

In all these movements they bring to the front, as the leading question in each, ***the property question,*** no matter what its degree of development at the time.

Finally, ***they labor everywhere for the union and agreement of the democratic parties of all countries.*** **"democratic parties"**

The Communists disdain to conceal their views and aims. They openly declare that their ends can be attained only by the forcible overthrow of all existing social conditions. Let the ruling classes tremble at a Communistic revolution. The proletarians have nothing to lose but their chains. They have a world to win.

WORKING MEN OF ALL COUNTRIES, UNITE! (The End)

For One World Government
(United Nations)

In 1992, the United Nations produced an "Agenda 21" for "sustainable development." The agenda's comprehensive plan of action is to result in global government by a small elite group. The plan is consistent with the Communist Manifesto. Links to the Agenda 21 document and websites explaining it are available online.

Note: Democrats including Representative Nancy Pelosi, Senator John Kerry, and Senator Harry Reid have spoken in Congress in support of Agenda 21 (AKA the Communist Manifesto of 1992).

President Obama's Communist Agenda

*Y*es Folks, we have a Communist in the White House. (If not, why are he, his community of czars, and the other Democratic Party leaders including Senate Majority Leader Harry Reid and House Minority Leader Nancy Pelosi demonstrably following the Communist Manifesto?)

Karl Marx, after assessing all of the parties of the day in 1848, selected the Democratic Party to advance the Communist agenda. Obama is the perfect President of the United States for Marx's Democratic party. Communism is so ingrained in him that he does not even know where it starts or stops.

On these pages I list President Obama's communist agenda, some of his presidential actions to achieve it, and pertinent explanatory and/or supportive text in the <u>Communist Manifesto</u>.

President Obama (and his czars):

1. Communist agenda: Destroy financial capital
run the debt up to undermine the soundness of the money/capital supply (the fastest way to destroy an advanced capitalist country).

Obama's actions
1) growing national debt by more than one trillion dollars a year;

2) not balking at the federal reserve's borrowing 43 cents of every United States dollar spent by the federal government from China, and other foreign countries, resulting in more and more tax dollars or percentage of gross domestic product leaving the USA to pay for the growing interest on the loans;

3) presented a Budget of the United States Government for 2012 with

increased spending based on a projected increase in individual income taxes from 956 billion dollars in 2011 to 1,145 billion dollars in 2012 and corporation income taxes from 198 billion dollars in 2011 to 327 billion dollars in 2012, numbers so unrealistic that not even a Democrat in congress would vote for it in February 2011 (note page 174 of the 2012 Budget);

4) preventing all efforts of the USA to become energy independent and stop the one way movement of United States money to fickle countries with oil when he: visited Brazil in April 2011 and encouraged them to drill offshore, assuring them that the USA "will be their best customer" while ordering federal agencies to effectively stop offshore drilling with red tape; delayed decision on construction of the Keystone XL Canada-to-Texas oil pipeline project until after the November 2012 election, in spite of the warning that Canada would turn to Asia to sell oil rather than wait on the pipeline (November 2011);

5) in summer 2011 and against the will of congress (that is the Republican majority in the U.S. House of Representatives) enacted "cap and trade" through federal orders which will result in higher utility rates, and threatens continued coal mining in the USA.

6) signed the Executive Order "Supporting Safe and Responsible Development of Unconventional Domestic Natural Gas Resources" April 13, 2012. This executive order gave him power over natural gas resources in the United States, that includes the control of the production of gas as well as the production and use of vehicles powered by the transportation fuel Compressed Natural Gas (CNG). With this executive order Obama can keep his promise that the U.S.A. will spread its wealth around (for example, Brazil and the Middle East) and can implement the United Nation's Agenda 21 (AKA "The 1992 Communist Manifesto"). Agenda 21 depicts the environmentalists' version of the Marxist "utopia" of communism. Its implementation is to result in a global society with a central government that dictates where everyone lives, what they eat, when they move, as well as what resources or energy sources they may use.

7) Democrats assumed total control of the budget process on January 3, 2007, when they took the House of Representatives as well as the Senate of Congress for the first time since 1995. (January 3, 2007 the deficit spending was declining for the fourth year in a row, the unemployment rate was 4.6%, and there had been 52 straight months of job growth). Continuing to ignore President Bush's requests, which totaled 17 since 2001, they failed to stop Fannie Mae and Freddie Mac's financial banking practices, and an economic meltdown occurred 15 months later. The U.S. government's budget is defined by the Federal Fiscal Year (FFY) which runs from October 1 of the prior

year to September 30 of the numbered year, so the budget for 2008 was from October 1, 2007 through September 30, 2008. The budget process is that the President submits the next year's budget for consideration by the first Monday in February and Congress has until September 30 to approve it. FFY 2008 Congressional Democrats compromised with Bush on spending. FFY 2009 Democrats bypassed Bush with continuing resolutions until Obama became president January 20, 2009 and signed off on their massive omnibus spending bill to complete the 2009 budget. Obama submitted budgets which predict unlikely high numbers for revenue collection to balance their spending. Since his budgets were not approved by the House of Representatives, the federal government is operating without a budget for the third year and going into the fourth. To accommodate fed's spending above intake of revenue, Congress raised the debt ceiling again and again rather than shut down the government's nonessential agencies. That resulted in the first downgrade of U.S. government debt in history. Standard & Poor's cut its rating of long-term U.S. Treasury securities by a notch from 'AAA' to 'AA+' August 7, 2011. International institutions continue to threaten more downgrading.

8) gave close to a billion dollars of taxpayer money to companies considered poor risk, that eventually went bankrupt, such as the alternative green energy company Solyndra, and to companies that used the money outside of the United States in England, Finland, China, and other countries.

9) reported by Fox News July 12, 2012 online "The U.S. budget deficit grew by nearly $60 billion in June, remaining on track to exceed $1 trillion for the fourth straight year. Through the first nine months of the budget year, the federal deficit totaled $904.2 billion, the Treasury Department reported Thursday. President Barack Obama is almost certain to face re-election having run trillion-dollar-plus deficits in each his first four years in office. . . . The International Monetary Fund warned that the U.S. economy could suffer another recession if Congress doesn't do something to avert the so-called 'fiscal cliff.'"

Explanatory/supportive text

from Section 1 of the Communist Manifesto:

The essential condition for the existence, and for the sway of the bourgeois class, is the formation and augmentation of capital.

2. Communist agenda: Encourage unhappiness worldwide

encourage unhappiness with and disapproval of the existing world order.

Obama's actions

1) did not condemn the president of Honduras for agitating for an unconstitutional 2nd term in 2009;

2) supported the plan for guns to Mexican drug lords with the allocation of $10 million in the 2009 American Reinvestment and Recovery Act (AKA Stimulus Bill) to the Bureau of Alcohol, Tobacco, Firearms, and Explosives for the ATF Project Gunrunner (AKA "Operation Fast and Furious");

3) ordered the expenditure of $20.3 million in "migration assistance" for Palestinian refugees and "conflict victims" in Gaza with ties to Hamas to resettle in the United States;

4) was hesitant to take sides on the revolution in Egypt (February 2011) or condemn the murder of anti government civilians in Iran (2009) and Libya (2011);

5) entered the conflict in Libya (March 2011) without consulting congress or seeking congressional approval;

6) signaled in his "Arab Speech" of May 19, 2011 that America is no longer Israel's guardian by stating that Israel's borders with a new Palestinian State would be the artificial and indefensible borders drawn by the United Nations in 1947 rather than the current ones in existence since Israel's defensive 1967 Six Day War;

7) June 2011 decided to formally resume contact with Egypt's Muslim Brotherhood, which does not recognize Israel, supports terror, and spreads hatred of the U.S. and Israel;

8) gave tacit approval to the organizers of Occupy Wall Street (started September 17, 2011) to continue their protests and interference with businesses throughout America;

9) sent a letter to Congress Fri. Oct. 14, 2011 informing them that he had sent U.S. troops to Uganda (who arrived Oct. 12) and will send others to South Sudan, the Central African Republic and the Democratic Republic of the Congo to put down years-long insurgencies, going against the traditional reluctance of the U.S. to intervene.

10) failed to condemn the mass persecution of Christians in the Mideast after saying in April 2012 "where we once were we are no longer a Christian nation, at least not 'just,' we are also a Jewish nation, a Muslim nation, and a Buddhist nation, and a Hindu nation and a nation of nonbelievers."

Explanatory/supportive text
from Section 1 of the Communist Manifesto:

All previous historical movements were movements of minorities, or in the interests of minorities. The proletarian movement is the self-conscious, independent movement of the immense majority, in the interests of the immense majority. The proletariat, the lowest stratum of our present society, cannot stir, cannot raise itself up, without the whole superincumbent strata of official society being sprung into the air.

Though not in substance, yet in form, the struggle of the proletariat with the bourgeoisie is at first a national struggle. The proletariat of each country must, of course, first of all settle matters with its own bourgeoisie.

In depicting the most general phases of the development of the proletariat, we traced the more or less veiled civil war, raging within existing society, up to the point where that war breaks out into open revolution, and where the violent overthrow of the bourgeoisie lays the foundation for the sway of the proletariat.

from Section 4 of the Communist Manifesto:

In short, the Communists everywhere support every revolutionary movement against the existing social and political order of things.

3. Communist agenda: Destroy credibility of capitalists
destroy the credibility of capitalists within the USA and around the world to decrease resistance to the new world order.

Obama's actions
1) apologized worldwide for the United States;

2) demonized Tea Party members (once known as the "Silent Majority" or taxpaying middle class) for unifying to protest the government's failure to follow the Constitution and stop the freefall in our economy with free market solutions;

3) does not act or follow through usually on his capitalist-like words from the TelePrompTer.

4) supported same-sex marriage. His explanation, quoted on May 10, 2012

54

White House Blog "President Obama Supports Same-Sex Marriage," did not include any reference to God, Bible, Judeo-Christian teachings, or any faith.

5) failed in spring 2012 to pressure Pakistan to free Dr. Afridi, imprisoned for working with the CIA to find and kill Osama Bin Laden.

Explanatory/supportive text

from Section 1 of the Communist Manifesto:

Modern industry has established the world-market, for which the discovery of America paved the way. . . .

has set up that single, unconscionable freedom -- Free Trade. In one word, for exploitation, veiled by religious and political illusions, naked, shameless, direct, brutal exploitation. . . .

The proletarian is without property; his relation to his wife and children has no longer anything in common with the bourgeois family-relations; modern industrial labor, modern subjection to capital, the same in England as in France, in America as in Germany, has stripped him of every trace of national character. Law, morality, religion, are to him so many bourgeois prejudices, behind which lurk in ambush just as many bourgeois interests.

from Section 2 of the Communist Manifesto:

There are, besides, eternal truths, such as Freedom, Justice, etc. that are common to all states of society. But Communism abolishes eternal truths, it abolishes all religion, and all morality, instead of constituting them on a new basis; it therefore acts in contradiction to all past historical experience.

4. Communist agenda: Promote dissatisfaction of working men and eliminate the middle class

promote working man's dissatisfaction with the capitalist or "ruling class" (middle class) so they eliminate it.

Obama's actions

1) are not helping in job creation in the private sector but rather are increasing the number of federal employees across the board, including requiring the hiring of 16,000 new Internal Revenue Service agents for implementation of the health care reform bill of 2010 H.R.3590 The Patient Protection and Affordable Care Act (also known as "Obamacare");

2) suppress the growth of small businesses by increasing regulations and operational costs ($1.7 trillion in 2010);

3) negatively impact the unemployment rate: reported as 8.2% for whites, 16.8% for blacks and 11.3% for Latinos in July 2011 (The New York Times September 2, 2011) and predicted by the Congressional Budget Office (September 2011) to be above 8% until 2014;

4) negatively impact unemployed Americans' job search and job change by extending weeks of unemployment benefits to years;

5) supported the Occupy Wall Street movement Fall 2011.

6) from 2007 (the year when Democrat Nancy Pelosi became Speaker of the House and pushed for spending over the federal budget) to 2010 virtually every American family's income and net worth declined according to the Federal Reserve Board's Survey of Consumer Finances. Families' mean income dropped 11.1% when adjusted for inflation and median income dropped 7.7%. Findings were reported June 16, 2012.

7) asked for more stimulus money and was denied by the House of Representatives following 2010 election wherein Republicans regained the majority in the house (but not the senate). Money from the stimulus 2009 American Reinvestment and Recovery Act was used in large part to shore up state governments and unions and it is gone. "Many public sector employees already have seen their wage growth slow or grind to a halt – even fall after adjusting for inflation" reported the Christian Science Monitor online July 12, 2012. The states of Arizona, California, and Florida are no longer giving raises. Due to increasing debt, U.S. municipalities like Stockton, California; Vallejo, California; and Jefferson County, Alabama are bankrupt. San Bernardino, California and Mammoth Lakes, California are on the road to bankruptcy. The mayor of Scranton, Pennsylvania—prohibited from filing bankruptcy by the state—is being sued for paying city workers, including him, minimum wage ($7.25/hour).

8) campaigning for reelection by:

a) promoting Marx's class warfare, that is, "you" are living poorly because "they" are living well, or in other words, "you" are losing your house because "they" are not paying their fair share in taxes;

b) denigrating successful middle class entrepreneurs with statements like the one he made extemporaneously at a campaign stop in Roanoke, Virginia Friday, July 13, 2012 (begin quote) There are a lot of wealthy, successful Americans who agree with me because they want to give something back. If you've been successful, you didn't get there on your own. You didn't get there on your own. I'm always struck by people who think, well, it must be because I was just so smart. There are a lot of smart people out there. It must be because I worked harder than everybody else. Let me tell you something -- there are a whole bunch of hardworking people out there. If you were successful, somebody along the line gave you some help. There was a great teacher somewhere in your life. Somebody helped to create this unbelievable American system that we have that allowed you to thrive. Somebody invested in roads and bridges. If you've got a business, you didn't build that. Somebody else made that happen. The Internet didn't get invented on its own. Government research created the Internet so that all the companies could make money off the Internet. (end quote);

c) dismissing criticizers through surrogates as "racists" or "protectors of the rich" and failing to address the merits of any criticism by making broad statements like the one he made on CBS news Thursday morning, July 12, 2012, "The mistake of my first couple of years was thinking that this job was just about getting the policy right, and, that's important, but the nature of this office is also to tell a story to the American people;"

d) blaming the bad economy on former President George W. Bush ("it was worse than I thought") or capitalism ("it never worked") and encouraging friendly news media to pile blame on Wall Street for illegal insider trading and other misdoings (media push cooled somewhat November 13, 2011, when the television program "60 Minutes" broke the story that elected officials had exempted themselves from the laws, and that House Majority now Minority Leader Nancy Pelosi used insider information that is illegal for the average citizen to trade with to purchase some very fruitful stock in Initial Public Offerings);

e) accusing Mitt Romney, the presumptive Republican presidential candidate for 2012, of sending jobs overseas or "outsourcing" because of his connection to Bain Capital (in the same years, 1999-2002, Obama was accepting campaign contributions from Bain executives) and Bain Capital's connection to an outsourcing investment company, Moduslink Global (Pelosi reportedly used the same company for some of her overseas investing). Yet Obama's stimulus 2009 Recovery Act outsourced taxpayer money to England, Finland, China, and other countries; Obama even outsourced the National Aeronautics and Space Administration (NASA) to Russia (Russia is paid millions of taxpayer dollars each time they transport a NASA astronaut to or from the space station). Per Obama's tax returns, he made: $1.6 million overseas in 2009 and paid $59,372 in taxes to foreign governments, $820,000 overseas in 2010 and paid $22,035 in foreign taxes, and $269,000 overseas in 2011 and paid $5,841 in foreign taxes; per his campaign committee's published report July 16, 2012, the Obama Victory Fund is fundraising in Geneva, Switzerland; Stockholm, Sweden; Paris, France; and (Communist) Shanghai, China.

9) promoting a welfare state:

a) Obama's stimulus 2009 Recovery Act increased the monthly benefit by about 15% through 2013 and made it easier for jobless, childless adults to qualify for the food stamp program or Supplemental Nutrition Assistance Program (SNAP). The number of people in SNAP has soared to an average 44.7 million in fiscal 2011 or 1 in 7 Americans, up 33% from fiscal 2009 (Obama is known as the Food Stamp or Entitlement President);

b) promoted and then signed The Patient Protection and Affordable Care Act AKA Obamacare which, as one of the largest tax increases in history, is blamed for the United States' worst economic downturn since the Great Depression, with flat to negative job growth in the private sector in the summer of 2012;

c) On July 12, 2012 Obama proposed welfare-to-work waivers for states— California, Connecticut, Minnesota, Nevada, and Utah expressed interest— which would in effect "gut" the 1996 law (welfare to work was at the heart of the landmark 1996 federal welfare reform law signed by Democratic President Bill Clinton, it replaced a federal entitlement with grants to the states, putting a time limit on how long families can get aid and requiring recipients to eventually go to work; the well liked program, now called Temporary Assistance for Needy Families, cut welfare in half when it started).

Explanatory/supportive text

from Section 1 of the Communist Manifesto:

The modern laborer, on the contrary, instead of rising with the progress of industry, sinks deeper and deeper below the conditions of existence of his own class. He becomes a pauper and pauperism develops more rapidly than population and wealth. And here it becomes evident, that the bourgeoisie is unfit any longer to be the ruling class in society, and to impose its conditions of existence upon society as an over-riding law. It is unfit to rule because it is incompetent to assure an existence to its slave within his slavery, because it cannot help letting him sink into such a state, that it has to feed him, instead of being fed by him. Society can no longer live under this bourgeoisie, in other words, its existence is no longer compatible with society.

5. Communist agenda: Use trade unions

promote trade unions because they upset/fight against the capitalist or "ruling class."

Obama's actions

1) announced that his agenda is the same as that of the Service Employees International Union (SEIU);

2) is pro "card check" so voting for or against unionization will no longer be done with a secret ballot;

3) is giving hundreds of waivers to trade unions so they do not have to adhere to his health care reform bill of 2010, H.R.3590 The Patient Protection and Affordable Care Act;

4) actively supported Democratic party organized union demonstrations in Wisconsin and Ohio March 2011;

5) ordered the National Labor Relations Board to prevent Boeing from extending its company to the right to work state of South Carolina from the union state of Washington May, 2011.

Explanatory/supportive text

from Section 1 of the Communist Manifesto:

But with the development of industry the proletariat not only increases in number; it becomes concentrated in greater masses, its strength grows, and it feels that strength more. The various interests and conditions of life within the ranks of the proletariat are more and more equalized, in proportion as machinery obliterates all distinctions of labor, and nearly everywhere reduces wages to the same low level. The growing competition among the bourgeois, and the resulting commercial crises, make the wages of the workers ever more fluctuating. The unceasing improvement of machinery, ever more rapidly developing, makes their livelihood more and more precarious; the collisions between individual workmen and individual bourgeois take more and more the character of collisions between two classes. Thereupon the workers begin to form combinations (Trades Unions) against the bourgeois; they club together in order to keep up the rate of wages; they found permanent associations in order to make provision beforehand for these occasional revolts. Here and there the contest breaks out into riots.

Now and then the workers are victorious, but only for a time. The real fruit of their battles lies, not in the immediate result, but in the ever-expanding union of the workers. This union is helped on by the improved means of communication that are created by modern industry and that place the workers of different localities in contact with one another. It was just this contact that was needed to centralize the numerous local struggles, all of the same character, into one national struggle between classes. But every class struggle is a political struggle. And that union, to attain which the burghers of the Middle Ages, with their miserable highways, required centuries, the modern proletarians, thanks to railways, achieve in a few years.

This organization of the proletarians into a class, and consequently into a political party, is continually being upset again by the competition between the workers themselves. But it ever rises up again, stronger, firmer, mightier. It compels legislative recognition of particular interests of the workers, by taking advantage of the divisions among the bourgeoisie itself. Thus the ten-hours' bill in England was carried.

Altogether collisions between the classes of the old society further, in many ways, the course of development of the proletariat. The bourgeoisie finds itself involved in a constant battle.

6. Communist agenda: Use socialists
ally with socialists to achieve similar goals.

Obama's actions
1) took over student college loans from banks;

2) bailed out and took ownership of automobile companies (2009);

3) signed into law H.R.3590 The Patient Protection and Affordable Health Care Act (2010), insuring: a fictional "all" (several million people are left out); future cost control; future access control; and destruction of free market health care with its accompanying research, innovation, price competition, and excellence (read Turner and others' 2011 book Why Obamacare Is Wrong For America: How the New Health Care Law Drives Up Costs, Puts Government in Charge of Your Decisions, and Threatens Your Constitutional Rights).

4) colluded with news media as evidenced May 22, 2012: Forty-three Catholic dioceses and organizations are suing the Obama administration in federal court over Obamacare's forcing religious institutions to cover contraceptives and drugs or devices to induce abortion under their health insurance plans. The popular media (ABC and NBC) blacked out the story on evening news while CBS gave it 19 seconds.

Explanatory/supportive text

from Section 4 of the Communist Manifesto:

The Communists fight for the attainment of the immediate aims, for the enforcement of the momentary interests of the working class; but in the movement of the present, they also represent and take care of the future of that movement. In France the Communists ally themselves with the Social-Democrats, against the conservative and radical bourgeoisie, reserving, however, the right to take up a critical position in regard to phrases and illusions traditionally handed down from the great Revolution.

7. Communist agenda: Eliminate international borders

eliminate international borders for one world government.

Obama's actions

1) is suing the state of Arizona to prevent enforcement of Senate Bill 1070 (passed in 2010), a bill to stop the uncontrolled drug and human smuggling from Mexico;

2) mandated the medical coverage of illegal immigrants in Obamacare (health care reform bill of 2010, H.R.3590 The Patient Protection and Affordable Care Act), the only low income people in the United States truly not eligible for already available state Medicaid or federal Medicare;

3) ended the three decade old National Aeronautics and Space Administration (NASA) shuttle program July 2011, making the USA dependent on other countries to take an American astronaut into space (e.g., $5 million to Russia per astronaut) and at risk of threat and intimidation from other countries (e.g., satellite weapons);

4) is destroying the integrity of U.S. citizenship when he:

a) promoted the Dream Act for legalization of illegal aliens, defeated by congress in 2010;

b) kept Immigration and Customs Enforcement (ICE) from deporting illegals for simply being in the U.S. illegally per ICE Director John Morton's memo June 17, 2011;

c) mandated a case-by-case review of over 300,000 illegals stuck in the federal court systems August 2011 (while waiting illegals can get work permits, jobs, free medical care and free food);

5) decided September 17, 2009 to scrap a missile-defense agreement negotiated by the Bush administration with Poland and the Czech Republic for mutual defense against a possible Iranian missile attack;

6) decided not to retrieve or destroy an intact, unmanned U.S. military drone with top secret technology that fell into Iran December 2011.

7) announced June 16, 2012 his Department of Homeland Security policy to allow young people who were brought to the USA as young children to be considered for relief from removal from the country or from entering into removal procedures (by selectively enforcing laws).

8) moving to shut down nine Border Patrol stations across four states. Fox News online reported July 11, 2012: "Critics of the move warn the closures will undercut efforts to intercept drug and human traffickers in well-traveled corridors north of the U.S.-Mexico border. Though the affected stations are scattered throughout northern and central Texas, and three other states, the coverage areas still see plenty of illegal immigrant activity — one soon-to-be-shuttered station in Amarillo, Texas, is right in the middle of the I-40 corridor; another in Riverside, Calif., is outside Los Angeles. U.S. Customs and Border Protection says it's closing the stations in order to reassign agents to high-priority areas closer to the border."

Explanatory/supportive text

from Section 2 of the Communist Manifesto:

The Communists are further reproached with desiring to abolish countries and nationality.

The working men have no country. We cannot take from them what they have not got. Since the proletariat must first of all acquire political supremacy, must rise to be the leading class of the nation, must constitute itself the nation, it is, so far, itself national, though not in the bourgeois sense of the word.

National differences and antagonisms between peoples are daily more and more vanishing, owing to the development of the bourgeoisie, to freedom of commerce, to the world-market, to uniformity in the mode of production and in the conditions of life corresponding thereto.

The supremacy of the proletariat will cause them to vanish still faster. United action, of the leading civilized countries at least, is one of the first conditions for the emancipation of the proletariat.

8. Communist agenda: Abolish private property

abolish private property because it cannot be possessed by all.

Obama's actions

1) bailed out and is currently maintaining two of the biggest players in the recent economic and financial debacle: Fannie Mae (FNMA - Federal National Mortgage Association) and Freddie Mac (a branch of the Federal Housing Administration [FHA] and US Department of Housing and Urban Development [HUD]). These two Democratic party sponsored enterprises intimidate mortgage lenders into giving people without collateral easy home financing, resulting in unpaid mortgages/property taxes and repossession of their homes/property by banks;

2) push to raise income taxes and estate/inheritance/death taxes;

3) authorized the Environmental Protection Agency's use of compliance order procedures that require virtually any landowner to pay hundreds of thousands of dollars in permit fees for ordinary home construction work or face hundreds of thousands of dollars in fines and penalties;

4) took over student college loans from banks;

5) will not support any curbing of frivolous lawsuits that result in high legal fees and loss of property for individual Americans and expensive defensive medicine by physicians.

6) June 16, 2012 it was reported that the Federal Reserve Board's Survey of Consumer Finances (a report issued by the Fed every 3 years) found that virtually every American family's income and net worth declined from 2007 to 2010 — years that coincided with Democrat Nancy Pelosi's leadership of the House of Representatives (wherein all bills for raising revenue originate) when spending over the revenue collected was approved which resulted in an unprecedented accumulation of debt and subsequent downgrading of the U.S.A.'s credit rating.

Explanatory/supportive text

from Section 1 of the Communist Manifesto:

The proletarian is without property;

from Section 2 of the Communist Manifesto:

In this sense, the theory of the Communists may be summed up in the single sentence: Abolition of private property. . . .Of course, in the beginning, this cannot be effected except by means of despotic inroads on the rights of property, and on the conditions of bourgeois production; by means of measures, therefore, which appear economically insufficient and untenable, but which, in the course of the movement, outstrip themselves, necessitate further inroads upon the old social order, and are unavoidable as a means of entirely revolutionizing the mode of production. . . . capital is converted into common property, into the property of all members of society, personal property is not . . . .

These measures will of course be different in different countries.

Nevertheless in the most advanced countries, the following will be pretty generally applicable.

1. Abolition of property in land and application of all rents of land to public purposes.

2. A heavy progressive or graduated income tax.

3. Abolition of all right of inheritance.

4. Confiscation of the property of all emigrants and rebels.

5. Centralization of credit in the hands of the State, by means of a national bank with State capital and an exclusive monopoly.

9. Communist agenda: Take control of communication and transportation

thwart the unfettered communication and urbanization needed by an advanced country/industrial nation and take control of communication, communicators, and transportation.

Obama's actions

1) included a federal allocation of $8 billion in the 2009 $787 billion Stimulus Bill for high-speed rail;

2) included a federal allocation of $7.2 billion in the 2009 $787 billion Stimulus Bill to expand broadband for internet access to the rural areas of Montana, Minnesota, and Kansas at a cost of $7 million per existing household (Mike Huckabee on Huckabee Fox News television show 7/9/2011);

3) included a "bridge to nowhere" in California in his budget proposal of February 14, 2011;

4) obtained "kill-switch" authorization from the Federal Communication Commission (FCC) to pull the plug on the Internet (as Hosni Mubarak did during Egypt's February 2011 uprising) with the FCC voting 3-2 along party lines for the Net Neutrality Act 12/21/2010 effective 2/21/2011;

5) signed March 16, 2012 the Executive Order "National Defense Resources Preparedness" under the Defense Production Act of 1950 giving him power to take over civil energy/transportation and to draft for military and nonmilitary purposes during war or peace.

6) signed April 13, 2012 the Executive Order "Supporting Safe and

Responsible Development of Unconventional Domestic Natural Gas Resources." This executive order gave him power over natural gas resources in the United States, that includes the government control of production or nonproduction of gas, and the control of the production and use of vehicles powered by the transportation fuel Compressed Natural Gas (CNG).

7) censored as well as colluded with news media as evidenced by: May 22, 2012 Forty-three Catholic dioceses and organizations are suing the Obama administration in federal court over Obamacare's forcing religious institutions to cover contraceptives and drugs or devices to induce abortion under their health insurance plans. Brent Bozell, President Media Research Center, reported that the popular media (ABC and NBC) blacked out the story on evening news while CBS gave it 19 seconds. A few news reporters recently confessed that they were pressured not to talk about concerns over the authenticity of Obama's birth certificate.

8) tightened control over the release of statistical data such as unemployment figures. Reported June 9, 2012 that journalists were ordered to remove their own telecommunications equipment as "Labor Department Forces Journalists to Use Government-Issued Computers."

9) signed July 6, 2012 the Executive Order "Assignment of National Security and Emergency Preparedness Communications Functions" giving him power to control all private communications in the country in the name of national security.

Explanatory/supportive text

from Section 1 of the Communist Manifesto:

The bourgeoisie keeps more and more doing away with the scattered state of the population, of the means of production, and of property. It has agglomerated production, and has concentrated property in a few hands.

from Section 2 of the Communist Manifesto:

Nevertheless in the most advanced countries, the following will be pretty generally applicable. . . .

6. Centralization of the means of communication and transport in the hands of the State.

9. Combination of agriculture with manufacturing industries; gradual abolition of the distinction between town and country, by a more equable distribution of the population over the country.

10. Communist agenda: Overthrow capitalists

overthrow the capitalists in power and install the proletarians "in the know" (AKA communists).

Obama's actions

1) *staffed his new White House administration in 2009 with more than 30 czars with far left and openly Communist backgrounds, using them rather than his congressionally vetted cabinet to plan and implement his agenda;*

2) *bailed out and took ownership of automobile companies (2009), "stiffing" or cheating the private investors;*

3) *signed into law* H.R.3590 The Patient Protection and Affordable Care Act (2010) *giving government control over 20% of the US economy with real time access to individuals' checking accounts for collection of payments and penalties;*

4) *(as a candidate Obama said in July 2008 that he wanted a "civilian national security force" that "would be just as powerful and well-funded as the U.S. military"), obtained funding for a civilian army in the middle of the health care reform bill in 2010 (see* H.R.3590. The Patient Protection and Affordable Care Act Sec. 5210. ESTABLISHING A READY RESERVE CORPS*);*

5) *signed New Year's Eve, 2011 the new National Defense Authorization Act (NDAA) allowing the U.S. military or a U.S. president to detain anybody anywhere indefinitely without trial for no reason so long as they say (not prove) you are suspected of terrorism; language excluding U.S. citizens was removed at Obama's request, so the privilege of the Writ of Habeas Corpus (Article I, Section 9, Clause 2 of the Constitution) to appear in public court to challenge the legitimacy of arrest and imprisonment is not allowed; and NDAA gives the U.S. military the power to conduct domestic anti-terrorism operations on U.S. soil, impacting the restraints on the military imposed by the Posse Comitatus Act (passed into U.S. federal law June 18, 1878).*

6) *signed March 16, 2012 the Executive Order "National Defense Resources Preparedness," under the Defense Production Act of 1950, giving him power to take over civil energy/transportation and to draft for military and nonmilitary purposes during war or peace.*

7) *signed April 13, 2012 the Executive Order "Supporting Safe and Responsible Development of Unconventional Domestic Natural Gas Resources" giving him power over natural gas resources in the United States, including the control of the production and use of vehicles powered by the transportation*

fuel Compressed Natural Gas (CNG) and government control of production of gas (or nonproduction per Agenda 21).

8) reauthorized funding and requested new regulations permitting and overseeing the development of domestic drone technologies. May 10, 2012 Public Radio International (PRI) online reported: "Domestic drones could enhance surveillance but infringe on privacy. Unmanned aerial vehicles commonly known as 'drones' may become a regular part of everyday life in the United States. President Barack Obama has reauthorized funding and requested new regulations permitting and overseeing the development of domestic drone technologies. As part of the FAA Modernization and Reform Act of 2012, signed into law by President Barack Obama in February, the Federal Aviation Administration is required to write new rules for expanding the use of U.S. airspace by domestic drones. Up until this point, drones were primarily operated by the military and homeland security forces. Hobbyists who were interested in building unmanned planes were carefully regulated. By <u>next week</u>, the administration will have to propose new practices to stimulate licensing for some government drones."

9) allowed Russians to participate in war exercises in the U.S.A. May 17, 2012 KRDO.com online reported: "FORT CARSON, Colo. - The Russians are coming - in fact, they're already here - but it may not be what you think. Twenty-two Russian army paratroopers are at Fort Carson for two weeks of training with the 10th Special Forces Group. The two nations' militaries have been conducting joint exercises for years, but U.S. officials say this is believed to be the first time Russian soldiers have trained on U.S. soil. The soldiers are training together on basic combat skills ranging from firing weapons to making parachute drops. It's the first step toward joint exercises in more complicated anti-terrorism operations. The training involves only unclassified weapons, and the Russians have U.S. escorts around the clock. U.S. soldiers are expected to go to Russia for similar exercises next year." Reports from other sources included that the Russians took and held the Denver Airport, had Nebraskan accented English, and were arriving in greater numbers and staying longer.

10) grew his community of czars to well over 100 in number by May 20, 2012 (which explains why his administration's tentacles are going out in so many more directions).

11) stopping different states' efforts to prevent voter fraud. Reported May 31, 2012 by the Miami Herald online: "Justice Department ordered Florida's elections division to halt a systematic effort to find and purge the state's voter rolls of noncitizen voters" claiming that "Florida's effort appears to violate both the 1965 Voting Rights Act, which protects minorities, and the 1993 National

Voter Registration Act -- which governs voter purges." July 10, 2012 Attorney General Eric Holder blocks South Carolina and Texas Voter Identification (ID) Laws on grounds of racial discrimination.

12) Obama's friendly exchange at the tail end of his 90 minute meeting with outgoing Russian President Dmitri Medvedev in Seoul, South Korea March 26, 2012 was picked up by hot microphones as reporters were let into the room for remarks by the two leaders. The actual exchange: President Obama: "On all these issues, but particularly missile defense, this, this can be solved but it's important for him to give me space." President Medvedev: "Yeah, I understand. I understand your message about space. Space for you…" President Obama: "This is my last election. After my election I have more flexibility." President Medvedev: "I understand. I will transmit this information to Vladimir." The incoming Russian President Vladimir Putin opposed the plan for deployment of U.S. missile defense interceptors and sensors in Europe. Seen together since, Presidents Vladimir and Obama "acted" unfriendly to each other.

13) failed to respond publicly to the encroachment of nuclear capable Russian bombers upon American airspace. Two incidents occurred in one month, the second on July 4, 2012. The following quotes are from the Washington Free Beacon online, and all were from the first half of 2012. February 14 "President Obama has ordered the Pentagon to consider cutting U.S. strategic nuclear forces to as low as 300 deployed warheads—below the number believed to be in China's arsenal and far fewer than current Russian strategic warhead stocks." June 26 "Russian strategic nuclear bombers threatened U.S. airspace near Alaska earlier this month and F-15 jets responded by intercepting the aircraft taking part in large-scale arctic war games, according to defense officials." June 28 "The U.S. Northern Command and joint U.S.-Canadian North American Aerospace Defense (NORAD) Command said two Russian bombers violated U.S. airspace near Alaska during recent arctic war games." June 29 "China's nuclear warhead stockpile is more than twice as large as U.S. intelligence estimates and could include as many as 3,000 warheads, according to a retired Russian general and former strategic forces commander." July 6 "Two Russian strategic nuclear bombers entered the U.S. air defense zone near the Pacific coast on Wednesday and were met by U.S. interceptor jets, defense officials told the Free Beacon." July 19 "Recent incursions into U.S. air defense zones by Russian nuclear bombers earlier this month were part of exercises that violated provisions of the 2010 New START treaty, according to U.S. officials."

14) had the Pentagon submit a heavily redacted report on China and its military capabilities to Congress. In an interview by Fox News July 13, 2012 over growing outrage on Capitol Hill over Pentagon cutting size of reports to Congress, Representative Buck McKeon, Chairman of the House Armed Services Committee, said "China just increased their spending budget over 12% while we are cutting a trillion dollars out of our defense budget." Report due March 1 per a law set in 2000 was received May 15. Last year's report was 79 pages, this year's 19 pages, and whole sections of last year's report were not in it this year. Explanation was that Pentagon briefers were told to limit reports to Congress to 15 pages to save money. Report cost $73,000 plus last year, $85,000 this year. Chairman McKeon sent a letter to Defense Secretary Leon Panetta asking him to change policy that "reeks of obstructionism, a lack of transparency, and is harmful to constitutionally mandated congressional oversight and national security." Rep. McKeon said that no funds will be approved "except for urgent needs for war fighters until they contact us and change this policy." In an email to Fox News, "McKeon's office said three sections of the 2012 China report that are required by law were missing and that it failed to mention major developments over the past year, such as the test flight of China's stealth jet, the J-22, and the maiden voyage of its first major aircraft carrier."

15) signing hundreds of executive orders, with restrictive and expensive rules and regulations for individual property owners, designed to bring about changes consistent with the UN's Agenda 21 map of the United States.

Explanatory/supportive text

from Section 2 of the Communist Manifesto:

The Communists are distinguished from the other working-class parties by this only:

(1) In the national struggles of the proletarians of the different countries, they point out and bring to the front the common interests of the entire proletariat, independently of all nationality.

(2) In the various stages of development which the struggle of the working class against the bourgeoisie has to pass through, they always and everywhere represent the interests of the movement as a whole.

The Communists, therefore, are on the one hand, practically, the most advanced and resolute section of the working-class parties of every country, that section which pushes forward all others; on the other hand, theoretically, they have over the great mass of the proletariat the advantage of clearly understanding the line of march, the conditions, and the ultimate general results of the proletarian movement.The immediate aim of the Communist is the same as that of all the other proletarian parties: formation of the proletariat into a class, overthrow of the bourgeois supremacy, conquest of political power by the proletariat. . . .

proletariat will use its political supremacy to wrest, by degrees, all capital from the bourgeoisie, to centralize all instruments of production in the hands of the State, i.e., of the proletariat organized as the ruling class; and to increase the total of productive forces as rapidly as possible. . . .

Nevertheless in the most advanced countries, the following will be pretty generally applicable. . . .

7. Extension of factories and instruments of production owned by the State; the bringing into cultivation of waste-lands, and the improvement of the soil generally in accordance with a common plan.

8. Equal liability of all to labor. Establishment of industrial armies, especially for agriculture.

11. Communist agenda: Revise history
revise history so people will forget it and not resist the new world order.

Obama's actions
1) cut off funding for the DC Opportunity Scholarship Program in May 2009, a popular voucher program for students in Washington, DC to escape failing public schools;

2) did not renew a $170 million 2-year program to fund Historically Black Colleges and Universities;

3) increased centralized federal control of education through increased funding with funding mandates in his budget proposal 2/14/2011.

4) aided the group that tried without success to revise U.S. history education in the 1990's to get a foothold with math and English. When offered a lump sum of money from the American Reinvestment and Recovery Act of 2009 (the Stimulus bill), 48 states (excepting Alaska and Texas) signed onto Obama's Race to the Top's Common Core State Standards Initiative authored by Achieve, Inc. Being implemented in Fall, 2012, Common Core standards will alter the math and English language arts standards of public schools' curriculums. English will be for reading instruction manuals rather than great literature, and college preparation for entering community college rather than university. Geometry will be taught by a method that has not worked in the past. Teachers are not permitted to deviate and tests will be constructed with the input of the Department of Education. Individual students' preferences or retention are not a consideration. States are instructed to compile and store data on students' test scores and ideally other data such as health history, family income and voter status. Sharing of data from state to state without parents' knowledge or consent is probable because of the department's recent gutting of federal privacy law. Achieve, Inc. "next generation science standards" is online July 10, 2012.

5) sent his deputies, House Minority Leader Nancy Pelosi and the White House Chief of Staff Jack Lew, following Supreme Court Chief Justice John G. Roberts Jr.'s decision to make The Patient Protection and Affordable Care Act (Obamacare) constitutional by deeming it a tax, to be interviewed on Sunday July 1, 2012 television and deny that Obamacare's individual mandate or "penalty on free riders" is a tax.

Explanatory/supportive text

from Section 2 of the Communist Manifesto:

In bourgeois society, therefore, the past dominates the present; in Communist society, the present dominates the past. . . .

The Communists have not invented the intervention of society in education; they do but seek to alter the character of that intervention, and to rescue education from the influence of the ruling class. . . .

Nevertheless in the most advanced countries, the following will be pretty generally applicable. . . .

10. Free education for all children in public schools. Abolition of children's factory labor in its present form. Combination of education with industrial production, &c., &c.

12. Communist agenda: Dominate world

acceptance of worldwide dominance by the communist party.

Obama's actions

1) is silent or deferring to the United Nations on international affairs (2009);

2) reported Arizona to the United Nations Human Rights Council (August 2010) for immigration law S.B. 1070, implying Arizona is under United Nations jurisdiction;

3) sought approval of the United Nations and not congress before sending soldiers to Libya (March 2011);

4) took "a back seat" to the United Nations in USA's "kinetic military action" in Libya (2011);

5) stated in a May 19, 2011 speech that Israel's borders with a new Palestinian State would be the borders drawn by the United Nations in 1947 rather than the current ones;

6) working for small arms/gun control through the United Nations. October 14, 2009: Obama reversed United States policy on a treaty to regulate arms sales by backing launching talks. The proposed Arms Trade Treaty would be a legally binding treaty tightening regulation of, and setting international standards for, the import, export and transfer of conventional weapons. According to Reuters, "the proposed treaty is opposed by conservative U.S. think tanks like the Heritage Foundation, which said last month that it would not restrict the access of 'dictators and terrorists' to arms but would be used to reduce the ability of democracies such as Israel to defend their people." July 2-27, 2012: The United Nations' conference in New York City is drafting a final version of the UN Arms Trade Treaty. If signed by the United States, the treaty will have the force of a constitutional amendment and override Amendment II of the Bill of Rights, the Right to Bear Arms.

7) signed January 18, 2011 Executive Order 13563 "Improving Regulation and Regulatory Review" which states "that our regulatory system must protect public health, welfare, safety, and our environment while promoting economic growth, innovation, competitiveness, and job creation. In an increasingly global economy, international regulatory cooperation, consistent with domestic law and prerogatives and U.S. trade policy, can be an important means of promoting the goals of Executive Order 13563." This executive order gave international regulatory cooperation priority over domestic laws and regulations.

8) sent delegation to Rio+20, United Nations Conference on Sustainable Development in Rio de Janeiro, Brazil, June 20-22, 2012 to discuss status of the United Nation's Agenda 21. Formally initiated by the United Nations' Kyoto Agreement in 1992, Agenda 21 is an eco-Marxist plan for one world government (AKA Communist Manifesto of 1992). In line with it, Obama signed Executive Order 13575 on June 9, 2011 establishing the White House Rural Council to "federally coordinate and implement environmental development locally in 'sustainable rural communities'" and Executive Order 13602 on March 15, 2012 establishing the White House Council on "Strong Cities, Strong Communities (SC2)."

9) planning (reported June 23, 2012) for the USA to sign the Land of the Sea Treaty (LOST), an "international agreement" ceding control of the high seas and ocean floor to an organization headquartered in Jamaica which calls itself the International Seabed Authority (ISA). A wholly owned subsidiary of the United Nations, the ISA will have the sole power and authority to issue "permits" for fishing and drilling and mining operations at sea. When globalists in the United States Senate introduced LOST 30 years ago, President Reagan said "No national interest of the United States can justify handing sovereign control of two-thirds of the Earth's surface over to the Third World."

10) realizing the Agenda 21 map of the United States for the United Nations, beginning in California where cities are on the verge of disappearing after going bankrupt in the summer of 2012 due to increasing debt, largely from union negotiated contracts for guaranteed job security, health care, and pensions.

Explanatory/supportive text

from the end of Section 2 of the Communist Manifesto:

In place of the old bourgeois society, with its classes and class antagonisms, we shall have an association, in which the free development of each is the condition for the free development of all.

from the end of Section 4 of the Communist Manifesto:

Finally, they labor everywhere for the union and agreement of the democratic parties of all countries. . . .

WORKING MEN OF ALL COUNTRIES, UNITE!

Note: President Obama deviates from the Communist Manifesto in one way. Karl Marx wrote near the end of Section 4 that "The Communists disdain to conceal their views and aims. They openly declare that their ends can be attained only by the forcible overthrow of all existing social conditions." Obama's deviousness is explained by Rules for Radicals: A Pragmatic Primer for Realistic Radicals, copyrighted in 1971 by Saul D. Alinsky, a book Obama was photographed explaining on a black board in a classroom some years ago.

From the Holy Bible, King James Version, the 1st Epistle of Paul the Apostle to Timothy, Chapter 2, Verses 1 & 2:

"I exhort therefore, that, first of all, supplications, prayers, intercessions, and giving of thanks, be made for all men;

For kings, and for all that are in authority; that we may lead a quiet and peaceable life in all godliness and honesty."

So I earnestly pray that President Barack Obama fulfills the oath he took before entering on the Execution of his Office, that oath being from the Constitution, Article 2, Section 1, [8]:

*   "I do solemnly swear (or affirm) that I will faithfully execute the Office of President of the United States, and will to the best of my Ability, preserve, protect and defend the Constitution of the United States." Amen.*

Constitution versus Communist Manifesto: The War Within America

With the Constitution as written, resolute Republican "Tea Party" perseverance in upcoming elections, and nonstop prayer, I believe that the United States of America can survive the current communist threat. The call has gone out for principled, united action by traditional and nontraditional Republicans who have not been permanently influenced by Democrats' past calls for "bipartisanship." But as in the past when there were grave challenges to the integrity of the United States, amendments to the Constitution are indicated.

1) A Balanced Budget Amendment

Congress is charged by the Constitution with the collection of taxes and payment of debts. As of December 2011, the USA is more than $48,000 per citizen and $130,000 per taxpayer in debt for a total of $15,000,000,000,000 and growing. Congress delayed discussion of the 2011 budget until after November 2010's elections. A Balanced Budget Amendment is needed to spur Congress to behave more responsibly.

2) The Equal Rights Amendment (ERA)

Its entire text as written in 1972 is:

Section 1. Equality of rights under the law shall not be denied or abridged by the United States or by any state on account of sex.

Section 2. The Congress shall have the power to enforce, by appropriate legislation, the provisions of this article.

Section 3. This amendment shall take effect two years after the date of ratification.

Some American Muslims are pushing their communities to let Muslim

Sharia law take precedence over local and state laws. The laws supporting equal rights that have passed and are currently proposed are not enough protection for women from this threat. The Equal Rights Amendment should be added to the Constitution as soon as possible.

3) Congressional Term Limits Amendment

Three (decreased from my first proposal for six when I was a candidate for the United States House of Representatives from the great state of Georgia in 2010) consecutive terms of two years for the House of Representatives and two consecutive terms of six years for the Senate.

Limiting terms will prevent career politicians from dominating Congress. Elections will be of more interest to constituents since they will not be able to rubberstamp their first choice indefinitely.

4) Official Language English Amendment

Living in Germany from 1975-7, I observed that persons in England, France, or Spain could not do business with each other or someone in Italy or Greece without an interpreter. Professional interpreters were usually proficient in 6 different languages. One of the greatest strengths of the United States is that someone in New York can phone someone in California, Hawaii, Alaska, or states in between and do business directly with them.

My best friend in high school in Niles, Ohio spoke just like me, but at home she spoke Italian (or "pig Latin" as she called it) with her parents who were immigrants from Naples. When I asked her how she did it she explained that she learned from her two older siblings (who were born in Italy) and in school. My friend went on to college and became a teacher of accounting.

We now have US citizens, born and educated in Atlanta, who cannot speak English. They will never achieve like my best friend did unless they learn English.

Stationed in Germany as an American soldier, I managed to work and live without speaking German. It was more time efficient to use the commissary for groceries and the base exchange for clothes at Ramstein Air Force Base. My friends and coworkers were American. Even though I lived "on the economy" away from the post, I, disappointingly, knew more German before I arrived in Germany than when I left.

Students' native languages should be used in our classrooms only to teach them English. Otherwise they will not have an equal opportunity to succeed.

5) Right to Privacy Amendment

Amendments 1, 3, and 4 of the 1st ten amendments (the Bill of Rights) protect privacy. Amendment 9 makes it clear that the Constitution does not specifically address every right retained by the people. Taken together Amendments 1, 3, 4, and 9 are known as the "penumbra," a shaded gray area of the Constitution that supports an unspecified but built-in or implicit right to privacy. "The concept of the privacy right 'penumbra' has informed many landmark Supreme Court decisions" (page 115, The United States Constitution: A Graphic Adaptation). With the advent of new technology and threats, this right is in jeopardy and should be made explicit.

6) An amendment to repeal the 1st sentence in the 1st section of the 14th Amendment,

proposed on June 13, 1866 and ratified on July 9, 1868 to provide citizenship to former slaves and their children: "All persons born or naturalized in the United States, and subject to the jurisdiction thereof, are citizens of the United States and of the State wherein they reside."

Repealing this statement will discontinue the birthright citizenship of children born in the United States to illegal immigrants.

7) An amendment to repeal the 16th Amendment

proposed on July 12, 1909 and ratified on February 3, 1913 for income taxes: "The Congress shall have power to lay and collect taxes on incomes, from whatever source derived, without apportionment among the several States, and without regard to any census or enumeration."

The purpose of this confiscatory income tax, like all of the strategies listed by Karl Marx in section 2 of The Communist Manifesto of 1848 ("revolutionizing . . . . the most advanced countries . . . . 2. A heavy progressive or graduated income tax"), is the "Abolition of private property."

I prefer the consumption tax known as the FairTax to the flat tax, because the implementation of the flat tax would still require an Internal Revenue Service. However, either is far superior to what we have now.

8) An amendment to repeal the 17th Amendment

(a progressive era amendment like the 16th) proposed on May 13, 1912 and ratified on April 8, 1913 for senators to be elected directly by the people rather than by their state legislatures. Federal interference/mandates to the states are wildly inappropriate, and they should be checked and balanced by state representation in the senate as intended by our founders. If senators were elected by state legislatures again, they would not be afraid to reign in entitlement programs that are bankrupting their states.

Rise Up Patriots! Let the Silent Majority Be Heard In 2012

Posted March 29, 2012 on Obama's Iron Curtain / Blog @ http://dianevann. authorsxpress.com

ALL PATRIOTS MUST WAKE UP NOW BEFORE NOVEMBER 2012 OR IT WILL BE TOO LATE!!!

We American voters are responsible for our political leaders. Because we became complacent and went to sleep our government has slid away from the Constitution towards the Communist Manifesto. Preservation of our liberty by adherence to the Constitution is the responsibility of each and every freedom loving American. If we do not pass it on to our descendants it is our fault. The call is out now for the silent majority of taxpaying, hardworking Americans to become politically active without delay.

The Democratic Party embraced Socialists and Communists long ago. Because of "bipartisanship" many Republicans in the Grand Old Party (GOP) have been corrupted. But the Republican Party, started by people like Frederick Douglass and Abraham Lincoln to prevent the spread of slavery, is still our natural home.

Activism at the grassroots level is critical in the next election. ACORN Alinskyites now running Occupy Wall Street are counting on stealing votes in the next election. "Secret shoppers" are looking to start lawsuits against states that require voters to show identification, so they can have "provisional votes" which they intend to count immediately in spite of any legally specified delay. Check out the website www.truethevote.org online and do what you can to educate and motivate other legitimate voters. Know your neighborhoods so you can challenge votes attributed to unoccupied houses.

The "normalcy bias" kept Jews from escaping Nazi* Germany when they saw their fellow Jews disappearing. We need to break through our own "normalcy bias" before this coming election or it will be too late. Our republic will descend into a Communist dictatorship if our negligent complacency continues through the elections of November 2012. The call

79

has gone out for principled, united action by traditional and nontraditional Republicans. Please answer it by joining and becoming active in your local GOP organization today. Tomorrow is not just another day.

*Nazi: abbreviation representing pronunciation of first two syllables of Nationalsozialistische (Partei); a member of the former National Socialist German Workers' party, founded on fascist principles in 1919, headed by Hitler from 1921. (Definition from Webster's New Collegiate Dictionary, 1953, G. & C. Merriam Co., Springfield, Mass.).

Posted April 13, 2012 on Obama's Iron Curtain/Blog@ http://dianevann.authorsxpress.com

Abortion is to Communism like a Headache is to a Brain Tumor

In his manifesto Marx wrote "The bourgeois . . . hears that the instruments of production are to be exploited in common, and, naturally, can come to no other conclusion than that the lot of being common to all will likewise fall to the women. He has not even a suspicion that the real point is to do away with the status of women as mere instruments of production" (p. 35, How the Communist Manifesto of 1848 Blueprints the Actions of the Democratic Party and President Obama Today). In fact, the Communists did treat women like prostitutes when they came into power in Russia in 1919. All women became the property of the nation instead of private property by decree. A certificate issued to a working class man by his union entitled him to make use of a "nationalized" woman between 17 and 32 years old. Some Communist leaders advocated complete replacement of marriage and family by promiscuity (more about this on page 72, The Naked Communist by W. Cleon Skousen, 1958). With that mentality, support of all abortion as well as infanticide comes naturally to a communist (witness China and Obama when he was in the Illinois state legislature). That kind of mentality is also present in America at the Democrats' sponsored Planned Parenthood facilities. According to witnesses, Planned Parenthood personnel act like abortion is just another form of birth control, so their clients will return to them three or four more times.

Posted November 7, 2012 on Obama's Iron Curtain/Blog@ http://dianevann.authorsxpress.com

How do you reconcile yourself with a nation that just sold its children into slavery?

The United States is $16 trillion in debt to nations and individuals worldwide. The president responsible for almost half of it with plans to spend more was just reelected. What collateral do you think he put up for that borrowing?

Recommended Reading and References

W. Cleon Skousen, *The Naked Communist*, (Salt Lake City: Ensign Publishing Company, 1958) Library of Congress Catalog Card Number: 58-14464.

K. Carl Smith with Dr. Karnie C. Smith, Sr., *Frederick Douglass Republicans: The Movement to Re-Ignite America's Passion for Liberty*, (Bloomington: Authorhouse, 2011) ISBN: 978-1-4567-5814-1 (e), Library of Congress Control Number: 2011905012.

Grace-Marie Turner, James C. Capretta, Thomas P. Miller, Robert E. Moffit, *Why Obamacare Is Wrong For America: How the New Health Care Law Drives Up Costs, Puts Government in Charge of Your Decisions, and Threatens Your Constitutional Rights*, (New York: HarperCollins, 2011) ISBN: 978-0-06-207601-4.

Joseph Katz, ed., *The Communist Manifesto, Karl Marx and Friedrich Engels; the Revolutionary Economic, Political, and Social Treatise That Has Transfigured the World*, (New York: Pocket Books, 1964) ISBN: 13: 978-0-671-67881-4 and 10: 0-671-67881-7.

Rius, *Marx For Beginners*, (New York: Pantheon Books, 1979) ISBN: 0-375-71461-8.

Jonathan Hennessey, Aaron McConnell, *The United States Constitution: A Graphic Adaptation*, (New York: Hill and Wang, 2008) ISBN: 13:978-0-8090-9470-7 and 10: 0-8090-9470-3.

Charlotte Thomson Iserbyt, *The Deliberate Dumbing Down of America: A Chronological Paper Trail*, (Ravenna: Conscience Press, 1999) ISBN: 0-9667071-0-9, Library of Congress Catalog Card Number: 98–89726.

About the Author

Diane Vann, RN graduated with a B.S.N. from the University of Nebraska Medical Center, Omaha, Nebraska in 1974 and M.S.N. from the University of Tennessee, Knoxville in 1986. She is married with no children. Her primary interests are nursing and health promotion. She is a Frederick Douglass Republican.

In an advertisement in weekly and daily newspapers January, 2010, paid for by her, in which she announced her candidacy in the Republican primary for the U.S. Congress, House of Representatives, 8th District, Georgia, she wrote "that President Obama is a run-of-the-mill communist who has cloaked himself in a 'second Messiah' kind of mystique. She recommends that Americans read for themselves the 'Communist Manifesto' or 'Manifesto of the Communist Party' written by Karl Marx in 1848 and contrast it to our 'Declaration of Independence,' the 'Constitution of the United States of America' and the 'Gettysburg Address.'" She writes this book as an aid for fulfilling that objective.

Made in the USA
Lexington, KY
19 March 2014